JANAMSAKHIS

JANAMSAKHIS
AGELESS STORIES, TIMELESS VALUES

Harish Dhillon

HAY HOUSE INDIA
New Delhi • London • Sydney
Carlsbad, California • New York City

Hay House Publishers (India) Pvt Ltd
Muskaan Complex, Plot No. 3, B-2, Vasant Kunj, New Delhi – 110070, India

Hay House LLC, P.O. Box 5100, Carlsbad, CA 92018-5100, USA
Hay House UK Ltd, The Sixth Floor, Watson House, 54 Baker Street, London W1U 7BU, UK
Hay House Australia Publishing Pty Ltd, 18/36 Ralph St., Alexandria NSW 2015, Australia

Email: contact@hayhouse.co.in
Website: www.hayhouse.co.in

Copyright © 2015 Harish Dhillon

Cover image, Janam-sākhī, CC BY-SA 4.0

The views and opinions expressed in this book are the author's own and the facts are as reported by him. They have been verified to the extent possible, and the publishers are not in any way liable for the same.

All rights reserved. No part of this publication may be reproduced, by any mechanical, photographic, or electronic process, or in the form of a phonographic recording, nor may it be stored in a retrieval system, transmitted, or otherwise be copied for public or private use – other than for "fair use" as brief quotations embodied in articles and reviews – without prior written permission of the publisher.

Sardar Sobha Singh Art Gallery, Andretta, Himachal Pradesh
(All the pictures used in this book are originally in colour, which have been converted into black and white for printing purposes.)

While every effort has been made to trace copyright holders for some of the pictures used inside this book, this has not been possible in all cases. Any omissions brought to our notice will be incorporated in the next edition and due credit will be given.

First Hay House India edition, 2015

ISBN: 978- 93-88302-46-3
ISBN: 978-93-84544-84-3 (e-book)

To
my granddaughter Inaaya and grandson Rehaan, five and three years old, respectively

In the hope that, when they are old enough to read, they will recognize and admire my ability to tell a good story and appreciate the fact that this book was written specially for them

The publisher and the author are greatly beholden to:

Bibi Gurcharan Kaur, daughter of Sardar Sobha Singh, for allowing the use of his paintings inside this book.

Contents

Introduction	9
Chapter 1 The Sacred Thread	17
Chapter 2 Sacha Sauda	27
Chapter 3 The Guru and the Qazi	47
Chapter 4 Bhai Lalo	59
Chapter 5 Haridwar and Ganga	83
Chapter 6 The Two Shopkeepers	93
Chapter 7 The Kumbh Mela	109
Chapter 8 Bad Village, Good Village	121
Chapter 9 The Story of the Needle	137
Chapter 10 The Faqir's Curse	151

Contents

Chapter 11 The Bowl of Milk and the Jasmine Petal	177
Chapter 12 The Brahmin and His 'Kitchen'	191
Chapter 13 The Joy of Giving	203
Chapter 14 The Abode of God	213
Chapter 15 Music and Worship	225
Chapter 16 The Widow and Her Lost Son	235
Chapter 17 Moola Keer and the Jewel Thief	251
Chapter 18 The Impostor	265
Chapter 19 Mud that Turned to Saffron	273
Chapter 20 There Is No Hindu, No Mussalman	285
Notes and References	289
Further Reading	297
Acknowledgements	299

Introduction

The Janamsakhis are cycles of tales purportedly drawn from the life of the first Guru of the Sikhs, Guru Nanak (1469–1539), as an attempt to compile popular stories connected with his life. These are not designed as biographies, nor can they strictly be called fables or parables, yet they do serve the same purpose – to preach a moral or illustrate an essential part of the Guru's life and his teachings.

There are four extant sets of tales: the Bala Janamsakhis, the Puratan Janamsakhis, the Meheraban Janamsakhis and those written supposedly by Bhai Mani Singh, an eighteenth-century Sikh scholar and martyr. He had been the childhood companion of Gobind Singh, the last Sikh Guru. Some of the stories are common to all the sets while some feature only in one set.

The writers of these tales drew on two sources: Guru Nanak's Bani also known as Gurbani or the voice of the Guru (which was compiled as part of the Adi Granth by Guru Arjan Dev, the fifth Guru, in 1604) and the first *var* (ballad) of Bhai Gurdas. Bhai Gurdas, the scribe of the Adi Granth when it was first compiled, was the nephew of Guru Amar Das, the third Guru, and was also a close associate of Baba Budha, who had been both an eyewitness and a party to the growth and development of the Nanak tradition.

INTRODUCTION

Unimpeachable as both these sources were, confusion arose from the fact that Bhai Gurdas' *var* provided sketchy biographical material, which did not satisfy the creative needs of the writers of the Janamsakhis. Thus they used their creativity to build on this material. For instance, Bhai Gurdas states simply that Nanak visited all the Hindu places of pilgrimage. The writers of these stories used their imagination to develop detailed accounts of Nanak's purported visits to places like Haridwar, Prayag (now Allahabad), Benaras (now Varanasi), Ujjain, Kurukshetra and Jagannath Puri.

However, this resulted in many versions of the same story and also led to contradictions and anachronisms. For example, in the Puratan Janamsakhis the story about Guru Angad's anointment as the second Guru has Gorakhnath, the founder of the Nath sect of yogis, in conversation with Guru Nanak. Historically, Gorakhnath lived and preached long before Nanak's time (in the eleventh century).

The Sakhis (which literally means stories) do not form any part of formal Sikh religious texts, largely because many of them are apocryphal. Another reason why they are not treated with much seriousness is the fact that they are replete with the supernatural and miracles. They were written long after the incident took place and based, as they were on oral history, the originals were coloured with the hues of personal interpretations of the person who wrote down the Janamsakhis.

These stories were created for anyone and everyone who believed in the supernatural and who had an implicit belief in the miracles that were said to have been performed. Hence, these miraculous stories, magnificent as they are, do what all stories about miracles do: hide more than they reveal, and Guru Nanak becomes more a symbol than a human being. Despite Guru Nanak's clear and emphatic disavowal of the miraculous, the Janamsakhis draw upon miracles and demand a belief in them as a commitment to faith. However, today, with the spread of education and development of a scientific bent of mind, these stories do not find a ready acceptance, primarily because their supernatural content has been discounted.

Modern scholars, on studying the genesis of the Janamsakhis, cast further doubts because these stories were not always rational and consistent and were often a product of legend and tradition, without any historical basis or proof. Hence, the veracity of the entire cycle of stories in the very popular Bala Janamsakhis became suspect. They claimed to be eyewitness accounts, though it was proved that Bala was not a contemporary of Guru Nanak. He lived long after and was a disciple of Baba Hindal, a dissenter. Thus, confusion over the fact whether Bala was a contemporary of Guru Nanak or not continues.

As the Sikh scholar, Dr Kirpal Singh, sums up, in his brilliant book, *Janamsakhi Tradition – An Analytical Study*:[1] 'The concept of authentic history began to emerge slowly out of the sea of fables and, gradually, things that appeared natural and acceptable to older generations became incredible or improbable to the younger generations.'

Till about fifty years ago, the Janamsakhis were kept alive by way of grandmothers narrating these stories to their grandchildren. However, with the advent of television, computers and the Internet, and with the break-up of the

INTRODUCTION

nuclear family, the entire tradition of oral storytelling has become a thing of the past. Today, these exist, if at all, only as stories in heavily illustrated children's books or as points of reference in research works on Guru Nanak.

However, they must not be forgotten. We must consider, as Dr Kirpal Singh points out, that the purpose of the Janamsakhis was perhaps not to record history or to provide an exegesis of Guru Nanak's Bani. The purpose was simply to reveal to the readers the wonderful personality of Guru Nanak and to provide information, in simple terms, of the unique and enlightened faith that he preached about.

Guru Nanak, as we know, was no unworldly mystic, floating above ordinary human beings in a smug aura of holiness. He was a man with his feet rooted firmly on the ground, a householder in every sense of the word, who, in a world fouled by hatred and violence, brought a message of peace and harmony to believers of the mutually hostile religions of Islam and Hinduism. Like Jesus Christ and Prophet Muhammad before him, Guru Nanak was impelled by a strong sense of social justice and equality. Like them, he emphasized direct access to divinity (without any middlemen) and challenged the established power structure through the way of life he asked his disciples to lead. He was, in his own gentle way, a crusader against corruption and social inequality. He always took the side of the poor, the marginalized and the exploited. He said that all men and women were equal, irrespective of caste, creed, wealth, social standing and gender. He taught that the basics of a good life were: honest earning through one's labour; concern and compassion for the less fortunate; selfless service to the community; and the constant renewal of faith in God through prayer. In spite of all the contradictions and conflicts, there can be no doubt of the essential veracity of the picture of Guru Nanak that emerges from the Janamsakhis.

I have retold some of the stories of the Janamsakhis, stripping them of all supernatural elements, including miracles. I could not find any reference to two of the stories – The Joy of Giving and The Widow and Her Lost Son – which I often used to hear in my childhood during sermons at different religious functions, and was influenced by, but have included them in this volume.

I have used my imagination to build up details of backgrounds, settings, incidents and even characters. I make no apology for taking such a liberty, for this is what happened to the Janamsakhis each time they were retold and when they were finally written. I have placed the stories against the background of Guru Nanak's *udasis* (travels) in order to give them a setting both in time and place.

Though this collection can never replace the warmth and affection of grandmothers' bedtime narrations, I sincerely hope it would be a fairly close substitute and would go a step further in bringing adult readers of all faiths closer to the teachings of Guru Nanak and, through them, to the essentials of living a good and fulfilling life.

Make compassion the cotton, contentment the yarn,
Continence the knot and purity the twist.
Such is the true sacred thread of the self.
Thou Brahmin-priest! Put this on me, shouldn't thou have it.
This thread neither snaps nor is soiled;
Neither burnt [nor] lost.
Sayeth Nanak: Blessed are the beings that around their neck put this.

— *Raga Asa* 471[2]

Chapter 1

THE SACRED THREAD

During ancient times, India was famous for its fabled wealth and many were the myths and legends that were propagated about it. Those who heard them coveted this wealth and were tempted to come to the country they called *sone ki chidya* (the golden bird) to see if they could lay their hands on some of it. Thus, Hindustan saw wave after wave of conquerors – first, the Aryans and then one after the other, the Greeks, the Bactrians, the Scythian tribes and the Huns. After the beginning of the eleventh century, came the tribes who differed greatly from one another but had one common factor: their religion, namely, Islam. The Ghaznavis, the Ghoris and the Tughlaqs helped themselves to much of Hindustan's fabled wealth and ruled for a while.

Since Punjab in the north was the gateway to India, it bore the brunt of all these invasions – its fate at the hands of the conquerors being best represented by the village of Talwandi, which lay between the rivers Ravi and Chenab, directly in the path of the armies that had set their eyes on Delhi. Thirteen times was the village of Talwandi destroyed and thirteen times – like the fabled phoenix – it rose again from its ashes. Its last rebirth took place under the supervision of Rai Bhoe, a Bhatti Rajput, who had converted to Islam. This too was representative of the times, because the Muslim conquerors, once they had settled down in the Punjab region, directed most of their energies towards either converting the kafirs or non-believers or destroying them.

For over three hundred years, Islam and Hinduism existed side by side in the Punjab region in a state of constant conflict. Hinduism had a pantheon of Gods and Goddesses who could be worshipped as idols and a society that was firmly based on the caste system. Islam believed firmly in monotheism, abhorred idolatry and had no caste system.

There were some attempts to bridge the divide between the two faiths. The Bhaktas[3] preached that there was only one God and he was without form. They advocated that all human beings were equal and preached against the caste system.

On the other side, for the first time, a Muslim sect called the Sufis introduced music as an integral part of the practice of Islam, very much like the singing of bhajans – religious songs – by the Hindus. They welcomed non-believers, both into their homes and their mosques, and advocated that all human beings had a right to observe their own form of worship. But any popular acceptance that these two tentative attempts at bridging the divide may have gained was destroyed by the Turko-Mongolic conqueror Taimur's (historically known as Tamerlane) invasion of India in 1398. The Muslim ruling class once again turned to killing and forcibly converting the

Hindus, destroying their temples and confiscating their property, both movable and immovable. They did this in the mistaken belief that through this destruction and conversion they were earning merit in the eyes of God.

Religious practice in both religions degenerated into the performance of empty rites and rituals. The Muslims believed that circumcision, abstinence from pork and alcohol and fasting during the holy month of Ramadan – the ninth month of the Muslim year, when Muslims fast between sunrise and sunset – were the only attributes of good Muslims.

The Hindus, determined to maintain their identity, turned to idol worship with a greater vengeance and an even more sustained belief in the caste system and the rituals of washing away their sins in the holy rivers, eating vegetarian food and wearing a thread on their torso to project themselves as superior. There was immense hostility and bitterness among the people of the two faiths, often resulting in clashes, in which the Muslims, since they were the rulers, usually gained the upper hand.

In Talwandi, Rai Bhoe was fortunate to get the services of Shiv Ram, the head of a Bedi family (learned in the Vedas) as his accountant. So wonderful and fruitful was this relationship that Shiv Ram's son, Kalyan Chand Das Bedi, succeeded him as accountant of the Bhatti family, now headed by Rai Bhoe's son, Rai Bular. On 14 April 1469 Kalyan Chand Das

Bedi, or Mehta Kalu as he was affectionately called, was blessed with a son who was named Nanak.

At Nanak's birth, Pandit Hardyal, the village astrologer, predicted that he would be a great man. But as Nanak grew from infancy to childhood, there was no indication of this predicted greatness whatsoever. He was a gentle, cheerful child, who happily shared his food and his toys with others but there was nothing that could be seen as a sign of future greatness.

However, once he started going to school, his performance was marked by a brilliance that had never before been seen in any child in Talwandi, a brilliance that could only be God-given. He was a prodigy in every sense of the word. He had the ability to compose spontaneously long poetic works, which were full of references to the metaphysical. All the three teachers who taught him at various stages of his school life were deeply impressed, both by his brilliance in studies and his compositions. But Mehta Kalu could only feel a growing disappointment and despondency in his heart. He wanted his son to make a place for himself in the world, to find service with one of the important officials of the ruling class, and, for this, his brilliance in languages and his ability to compose verses would be of no use.

Nanak had developed a meditative nature and had begun to look for reasons for the schism between Hinduism and Islam. One of them was the insistence of the followers of each religion on practising rituals, which were often diametrically opposed to each other.

The Sacred Thread

Nanak was thirteen, an age when, according to tradition, he needed to begin wearing the *janeu* or the sacred thread woven out of cotton yarn and blessed by a priest according to rituals laid down by religious tradition. This cord is worn around the neck and looped over the shoulder by all Hindus of the upper castes for the rest of their lives. It is like a badge, marking the wearer as a member of the superior castes.

Pandit Hardyal was called to set an auspicious date for the ceremony and, once this was done, messengers were sent to friends and relatives to invite them to the function. Elaborate preparations were set in motion days in advance. A temporary platform of bricks and mud was built in the centre of Mehta Kalu's courtyard, which, shortly before the ceremony, had been purified with the plastering of a mixture of mud and cow dung.

On the chosen day, the courtyard was packed to capacity with friends, relatives and well-wishers. Pandit Hardyal sat in the centre of the platform with the young Nanak facing him: his legs crossed, his back straight, his body bare from the waist upwards. Hardyal started performing the rituals before Nanak was formally initiated – he lit lamps and burnt incense, a strong smell of which pervaded the air, drew the ritual symbolic figures with flour on the ground, chanted the ancient, prescribed mantras over the cocoon of cotton cord that he had brought with him so as to sanctify it. After doing all the preliminary work, Pandit Hardyal bent forward to put the cord across Nanak's chest but Nanak drew away from him and putting up his hand in indication for him to stop, asked: 'What is this?'

'You know what it is my son,' Pandit Hardyal said as gently as he could. 'This is the *janeu*, the sacred thread which marks you out as a member of the upper castes. By wearing it you will become a twice-born Hindu, a pure Hindu,' Pandit Hardyal added.

'Can the mere wearing of a thread put you in a higher category? It is not the mere wearing of badges and symbols that will mark us out as superior human beings or as pure Hindus, but it is our actions and our actions alone that will give us our positions in the hierarchy of men. Besides, what sanctity and superiority can this thread give me, which itself will in due course get soiled and break?' asked Nanak.

Pandit Hardyal was rendered speechless, his hands still holding the sacred thread, frozen in mid-air.

Nanak shook his head. 'No,' he said, his voice loud enough to be heard in the farthest corners of the courtyard. 'I will not wear a thread which encourages us in the false belief that empty rituals and rites are the way to salvation and makes us forget that the only road to it lies in the goodness of our actions and in compassion,' he finished.

Everyone there was shocked and there was a gasp of disbelief from the gathering, which had never witnessed such a blatant and gross act of sacrilege. They were sure that Nanak's wayward behaviour would draw the wrath of the Gods on the Bedi household. Those who knew Nanak, a quiet, meditative, soft-spoken boy, were even more shocked. No one had imagined that he was capable of such a strong and forceful expression of will.

Pandit Hardyal sat there, confusion writ large on his face. He could not condemn Nanak altogether because he knew there was much sense in what the boy had said – right action and compassion were far more important in gaining salvation than the wearing of the sacred thread or other religious symbols and the performing of rituals. Yet, he had never before faced such rejection of what had been considered sacred down the ages.

Mehta Kalu was of course mortified beyond words. He felt that he would never again be able to show his face to his kith and kin as his son had brought shame and humiliation upon the whole family. Nanak's act confirmed what had already become a fixed notion in his mind – his son would come to no good. During that long, pregnant silence, Nanak got to his feet, stood straight and erect, free of any sign of remorse and regret at what he had done, and went inside the house.

The guests, keen to get as far away as possible from the scene of this terrible sacrilege, went quickly away, with just a few taking the trouble to say goodbye to Mehta Kalu. Yet, there were many, who, while reflecting on Nanak's words in private, admitted that there was a great deal of truth in what he had said.

For Nanak, it was the beginning of a lifelong crusade against the performing of empty rites and rituals.

Make this frail body thy shop,
And stock it with merchandise of the True Name.
He is a successful dealer in horses
Who breeds the horses of truth,
And carries with him the haversack of virtues
As food stock for the journey.

– *Sorath*[4]

Chapter 2

SACHA SAUDA*

𝒯HE YEARS FLOWED ON, ONE INTO THE OTHER, AND soon Nanak was sixteen years old. The Janamsakhis tell us of Mehta Kalu's efforts to find a gainful and suitable occupation for his son. They tell us of the time that Nanak spent taking his herd of cattle out to feed in the pastures and also tell us numerous stories of the miraculous incidents that ensued.

These are obviously attempts to remind us that this may have been a phase in Nanak's life of very ordinary and humdrum occupation, but he was far from being an ordinary human being. We can presume that, alone in the mute company of his herd, he gave himself up to prayer and meditation.

The village of Talwandi may have been directly in the path of the conquerors on their way to Delhi (and it repeatedly

*The true bargain.

paid the price for this geographical accident), but it also lay in the path of numerous mendicants, sadhus and holy men of all shades and hues, who were making their way to the east or the south on various pilgrimages or to take part in various religious fairs organized across what was then Hindustan. Almost all of them camped in a grove of trees on the outskirts of the village and Nanak interacted with many of them and listened to their words of wisdom, pondered over them and became familiar with the faiths and beliefs of many different sects and orders, some of them bordering on the esoteric.

It was during these years that he became well acquainted with the dervish[5] Sayyad Hussain and gained an intimate knowledge of the Sufi line of thought and of the collection of parables through which the Sufis used to bring home their thoughts and beliefs to laymen. He was profoundly influenced by this line of thought and admired its philosophy throughout his life. The Sufis already had done what Nanak aimed at doing: They took the best aspects of Hinduism and Islam in order to reach God. The Sufis were revered by both Hindus and Muslims in India, and to this day the Sufi dargahs (shrines) stand testament to the fact.

Nanak had lost his restlessness ever since he began meeting the holy men and seemed content with his way of life and was more cheerful. Seeing him thus, his family and friends were also content. But Mehta Kalu was not. He saw no sign of the greatness that Pandit Hardyal had predicted for his son in the occupation of a cowherd. It was all very well for Nanak to compose reflective and meditative mystical verses, which impressed all who heard them (even the most learned scholars and the wisest of sages), but these would not bring him any worldly fame or wealth. The one plus point was Nanak's new-found docile frame of mind, in which he seemed to be at peace with himself and more receptive to what his father had to say to him. Sensing this, Mehta Kalu felt that it was perhaps time to launch his son in a more profitable and challenging occupation – trading.

Suitable premises were found from where Nanak could start his business with twenty silver coins, a large amount of money in those days. Mehta Kalu also gave him a list of commodities that were to be purchased from the nearby market town of Chuharkhana at wholesale prices, and sold at a premium in Talwandi, as they were in much demand in the village.

Mehta Kalu hoped that this would be the first step towards becoming a permanent occupation for Nanak. To provide some kind of security and support, Bala, a young boy from the Jat clan of the Sandhus, was found as a companion to accompany him. Nanak, however, suspected that Bala was being sent to also keep an eye on him so that he would not lose his focus.

Mehta Kalu accompanied the two boys for some distance, repeating instructions and giving advice on how Nanak could strike the most profitable and successful bargains. Among the plethora of instructions that he gave was the firm and clear one that they should take the most direct route, both while going to Chuharkhana and on the way back and avoid interaction with anyone. How little influence Mehta Kalu's words had on his son was shown the moment the father turned back towards Talwandi.

'Let us take the path through the woods. It is more picturesque and our journey will be more interesting and pleasant than if we take the thoroughfare to Chuharkhana,' said Nanak to Bala.

'You know what your father insisted upon: that we should take the shortest route to the market and you know very well that the path through the woods is much longer,' replied Bala.

Bala knew that Nanak's interest in the longer route lay in the hope of meeting some holy men in the forest. If they did find such men, Nanak would surely stop to talk to them and the discussion that ensued would be a long one. With these thoughts in mind Bala said to Nanak: 'You know you will be violating two of your father's most important instructions. You also know what will happen to us when he finds out that we disobeyed him.'

Nanak knew what would happen well enough. Before these last few more equable and quieter years, he could remember numerous occasions when his father had beaten him black and blue whenever he had disobeyed him.

'I know well enough and it does not frighten me. I will willingly pay the price for my disobedience. You can tell him that you did your very best to discourage me and begged me not to take the forest route but I did not listen. I promise I will bear witness to the fact that this is exactly what happened and take upon myself the share of punishment that would otherwise have fallen to your lot,' said Nanak while trying to convince Bala to take the longer route.

Bala was left with no arguments. As he followed Nanak, he prayed fervently that it would be one of those days when there were no sadhus, no swamis and no mendicants on the route and he and Nanak could walk through the forest without stopping. But his prayers went unanswered, because there were dozens of sadhus in the forest. Each had adopted a yogic *asana* or posture of his choice. Some sat in the lotus position, some stood on one leg, some with their arms stretched to the sides and some with their arms stretched over their heads. There were no prayers, no chanting of mantras or singing of bhajans – not even a dialogue or discussion between any of them. They all had their eyes closed, lost in their own private meditation, presenting a strange tableau to the young Nanak. Even though each of them had adopted his own special yogic *asana* for his meditation, they did have one thing in common – they were all naked, their bodies smeared with ash, and they wore their hair in long, matted deadlocks. They were the Nagas. Nanak had heard of this particular order of sadhus but he had never before met one and his knowledge of their practices and beliefs was limited. He was excited by the prospect of learning more about this esoteric sect.

He looked closely at each one of them and then zeroed in on the one who sat in the lotus position. He was obviously the seniormost, as far as age was concerned, but, more than that, there was an air of authority, of being in control, that he exuded even while involved in silent meditation. Nanak knew instinctively that he must be their leader. He took his place opposite the sadhu, assuming the lotus position too. Becoming aware of the presence of an intruder, the sadhu opened his eyes and looked fixedly at the boy. Nanak reached forward and touched the sadhu's feet.

'Forgive me, O holy one, for breaking in on your meditation,' said Nanak.

The sadhu held up his hand in blessing and asked: 'What is it? What do you want from me?'

'Your blessings of course,' Nanak answered and when the sadhu made no comment, he went on, 'I would also like to learn more about your beliefs and your way of life.'

The Naga smiled and said: 'My blessings you already have. About providing you more information about the Naga beliefs and way of life, I am not too sure even though I am the Mahamandleshwar* of my *akhara* – a place of practice with facilities for boarding, lodging and training – and in the best position to give you information.' He paused for a moment and then went on: 'Unfortunately, all our practices and beliefs are such closely guarded secrets, and our rites and rituals performed so firmly away from the gaze of others, that I don't think there is much that I can tell you.'

He saw the look of disappointment on Nanak's face and knew that the boy was genuine in his quest for more knowledge about the Nagas.

'You ask me the questions and I will answer the ones that do not impinge upon our code of secrecy,' said the sadhu.

---

*One who has been elevated by his peers to the highest level of spiritual guardianship.

Bala had by now reconciled himself to the situation and sat a few steps away, leaning his back against a tree trunk and listened in on the conversation that followed between the sadhu and his friend.

'Why do we see Naga sadhus so rarely? Even though I know of you, this is the first time in my life that I have actually come face to face with one,' queried Nanak.

'We like to keep to ourselves and our particular *akhara* is based in a group of caves in the Himalayas. The only time we descend to what you call civilization is once in four years when we proceed to take the holy bath at the Kumbh Mela.⁶ We are now on our way to Haridwar to take part in the *mela*, which is to be held there shortly,' replied the sadhu.

In the following one hour, Nanak learnt that the Nagas were a unique sect of Shaivite sadhus who belonged to the Digambar tradition of saints: they were skyclad. The tradition of the Naga sadhus, which exists to this day, derives its name from the word 'nag' which means 'naked' and they remain naked even in the coldest weather. They regard themselves as the representatives of Lord Shiva in this world and, to this end, they adopt certain characteristics of Lord Shiva's appearance. They smear their bodies with sacred ash, which is obtained by burning certain special ingredients and then purified with the recitation of special prayers and mantras over it. Their matted, uncombed hair can be seen either hanging down to their shoulders or coiled around their heads. The consumption of *bhang* or marijuana is considered an essential part of their rituals and it is very common to see a Naga sadhu carrying a *chillum* or clay pipe, which the Nagas call the Shiv Muli. They believe that consumption of *bhang* will be a tool, which will help them avoid worldly distractions and which will help them to be better equipped to gain total self-control. On evolving further they realize that they no longer need the aid of this intoxicant and it is abjured by the senior members of the *akhara*.

The origins of the Naga tradition are so old that they are lost in the mists of antiquity and the only certainty is that the sect was founded by the sage Dattareya.[7] They are ascetics who have renounced the materialistic world and taken the vows of celibacy in order to attain salvation, i.e., freedom from the cycle of birth and death. Because of the rigours of their lives and the extreme form of renunciation that they practise, the Nagas firmly believe that they have overcome their earthly existence and, in fact, often declare themselves as being dead.

The Nagas are also often referred to as Naga Babas or warrior ascetics. This name comes from the fact that the Shankarcharya[8] organized them as a militant force that would protect the Vedic religion. Their categorization into *akharas* is very much like the organization of the army into regiments. They are trained in martial arts and, when they move in procession under their Mahamandleshwar to bathe in the holy waters during the Kumbh Mela, they demonstrate these skills in performances, which evoke both admiration and awe in the beholders. But in spite of all this training and the tradition of being holy warriors, the Nagas are essentially a non-violent sect.

The Mahamandleshwar reiterated that all their rites and rituals were practised in strict secrecy and no outsider was allowed to even witness them, leave alone participate in them. Even the initiation of a new acolyte, which stretches over a two-day period, had never been witnessed by any outsider. He pointed out that because of the fact that they wore no clothes and because of their esoteric practices they were often misunderstood by the common people. But so complete was their renunciation of the world, that they were not concerned about what others thought of them.

'We have detached ourselves completely from the world and from material things. Just as we do not wear clothes, we also do not search for food. We eat whatever is provided to us,' said the sadhu.

'And if no food is provided to you for days?' asked Nanak.

'It does not matter. We have learnt to weather hunger just as we have learnt to weather the severe winter conditions that we live through,' replied the sadhu.

'When did you last eat?' asked Nanak getting curious.

'I do not remember, but it must be about a week ago,' replied the sadhu.

Nanak was shocked at the calm and matter-of-fact way in which the sadhu had made this statement.

'When did these other sadhus last eat?' Nanak's voice was scarcely more than a whisper, overcome as he was by the enormity of the difficulties that the Naga sadhus faced every day on the path that they had chosen to follow in their quest for salvation.

'None of them have eaten in a week. Some of them have gone without food for an even longer period of time,' answered the sadhu.

Nanak looked around once again and peered closely into the faces of the sadhus who were nearest to him. Now that he knew the truth, he saw signs of starvation in the faces that he looked into. He knew as a certainty that if these men did not eat soon some of them would die. He turned back to look into the Mahamandleshwar's face. The sadhu gave a warm, radiant smile and said: 'Come, my young friend. Unlike me, you are a man of the world and you have worldly occupations that you must attend to and wordly responsibilities that you must fulfil. You have tarried long enough here in the forest with men who are essentially dead. You must now return to the world of the living.'

Nanak rose from the ground and touched the sadhu's feet. The sadhu smiled at the boy and held up his hand in blessing.

Much to Bala's relief, it was as the Mahamandleshwar had said, there was little about the Naga order that he could share with this intense boy and the discussion was over well within an hour. They could now move onto Chuharkhana and get on with their business.

The two boys hurried on to the town and, as they entered the main market, they were besieged by the touts of the wholesale dealers offering them heavy discounts. Bala pulled out his list and began to consult it to see which shops they should go to. Nanak ignored both the touts and the list and, much to Bala's amazement, made it straight to the biggest wholesale grocer.

'Nanak,' Bala called softly and then, more loudly, once again, 'Nanak.' Getting no response he rushed after Nanak, caught up with him and held him by the arm and said: 'What are you doing here? We have no grocery items on our list.'

'We didn't before, but now they are our priority,' replied Nanak, with a sense of urgency in his voice.

For a moment there was a befuddled look on Bala's face and then understanding dawned on him. 'No,' he said sharply. 'You can't do this. For the very first time in your life, your father has reposed enough trust and faith in your abilities to ask you to do something worthwhile – to make a true bargain. I know that your heart goes out to those famished ascetics, but you cannot betray his trust,' added Bala.

He paused for breath and Nanak turned back to face the shopkeeper and began to list out the things he needed in order to feed the sadhus.

'I need flour, pulses, cooking oil …,' Nanak began listing the things he needed.

'How much of each item do you need?' asked the shopkeeper.

Nanak thought for a while and realized that he had no idea of the quantities involved in feeding those many men. He decided to let it rest on the experience of the shopkeeper.

'You will have to help me with this. I need enough food to feed fifty starving sadhus,' Nanak requested the shopkeeper.

Bala pleaded with Nanak: 'Please Nanak, please listen to me, I beg of you. You know how your father feels about you, the hostility and bitterness that he carries in his heart towards you. If you do this, the consequences will be terrible. Can we not at least make a compromise – spend five silver coins on buying food for your Naga sadhus and the rest on buying items from your father's list? This way you will have carried out a part of your father's wishes. He might even forgive you for the money you are spending on feeding the sadhus.'

Nanak came up with his signature smile, full of patience and serenity.

'You know that a compromise never satisfies anyone. You saw the condition of the sadhus and you still doubt that the only true bargain that I can make is to use all my money to feed them?' asked Nanak.

He paused to let his words sink in. 'Any dilution of my bargain will be a dilution of the truth. I will face the consequences of my actions, no matter how terrible they might be. It is God who leads me to do what I am doing and it is God who will help me to deal with the consequences. My father has sent me to Chuharkhana to make a true bargain. For him this means buying goods at a cheap rate and selling them at a higher one, thus making a respectable profit on the transaction. But the profit from this bargain will be mine and the bargain will thus be a selfish bargain that will benefit only me. On the other hand, there is a group of hungry sadhus on the brink of starvation, who have renounced the world and detached themselves completely from material needs. So absolute is their detachment that they do not even go out in search of food – they eat only when God provides them with food and they eat only what God provides. They would prefer to die of starvation than go in search of food. By using my money and efforts to feed these holy men, I will have become an agent of God and will have performed a truly selfless service. Tell me, which is a more profitable bargain: using the money to make a monetary profit for myself or using the money to perform an act in the service of God?'

Though Bala felt sympathy for what Nanak was about to do, he was worried about Nanak's father's reaction to the whole thing. He did not want to abandon his friend and go back to the village, but then neither would his fear of what would happen to Nanak let him be actively involved in what the latter was doing.

Nanak bought fresh vegetables and fruit and firewood. He asked the grocer to arrange two cooks, two porters and to loan necessary cooking utensils to him. Once these were arranged for, the little group made its way quickly to the grove of trees, with Bala trailing behind.

Fires were lit and the two cooks, going efficiently about their task, soon had the cooking well underway. Nanak, who understood his friend's dilemma, turned to him now and said as gently as he could: 'I worry about what my father will do to you when he finds out that you were with me through all this. Run back home, and if confronted, deny any knowledge of what I have done.'

Bala hesitated for a moment, knowing that, by going away now, he was in a sense betraying his friend.

'Go, my friend. I know what is in your heart and that is more than enough proof of your love and loyalty,' assured Nanak.

Bala hesitated a moment longer and then he ran quickly home and hid himself in the inner recesses of his house.

The evening shadows had begun to lengthen by the time the sadhus finished eating. Mehta Kalu was consumed with anxiety for his son's well-being. Nanak should have returned to Talwandi a long time ago. As the hours slipped away, he feared the worst: that someone in the market or on the way had abducted the boys to steal the money they were carrying. As the hours went by without any sign of the boys, he became more and more anxious for them. Again and again, he walked to the edge of the village and strained his eyes, peering in the direction of Chuharkhana to see if he could catch a glimpse of the boys on their way back home. But each time he returned home with a heavy heart.

Then the thought occurred to him that perhaps the boys had returned and were at Bala's house. He sent someone to look for them there. Bala's family, unaware that he was hiding in the house, sent back an answer that the boys had not returned. Much later, when the second emissary came, Bala, unable to restrain his curiosity, stole to the door to listen in to the conversation and was spotted by his mother. On being questioned, he confessed to what had happened. His father caught him by the ear and dragged him to Mehta Kalu's house.

At first, afraid of the consequences for his friend, Bala would not repeat what he had told his father. But when his father administered a couple of stinging slaps to his cheeks, Bala repeated the entire story, starting from the time they had strayed from the thoroughfare onto the bridle path through the forest. Mehta Kalu's face turned red with suppressed rage. Not only was he upset with what Nanak had done, but he was also angry because of the anxiety that his son had needlessly caused him over the last few hours. He strode from his house towards the forest.

Nanak had paid off the cooks and porters and requested them to carry the cooking utensils back to the grocer, then clutching the change that was left, he set out for Talwandi. He could not remember a time when he had felt happier or more fulfilled in his life. He came out of the shadow of the trees and stopped in his tracks, the song in his heart stilled: he had come face to face with his father.

Bala, in the meantime, his heart quaking with fear at what might happen to his friend, had run straight to Rai Bular's *haveli* (mansion). The Rai had heard about the bargain that Nanak had been sent to make and he had also heard the news of how late the boy was in returning to Talwandi. Ever since the sun had begun to set, he had paced restlessly up and down the courtyard of his house, stopping only to send someone to Mehta Kalu's house to find out if there was any news of the boy.

When Bala came in, worry and anxiety writ large on his face, and told Rai Bular the details of what had happened, he wrapped a shawl around his shoulder, more as a badge of his authority than as a protection against the chill of the evening and hurried towards the forest.

Mehta Kalu, on seeing his son, burst into loud and terrible expletives. He would have done worse, but Nanki, who had run behind her father, restrained him. Soon Rai Bular and Bala too reached the spot. Mehta Kalu kept repeating over and over again that Nanak was a failure; he could not carry out the first real task that had been assigned to him.

'I wash my hands off you. You will never be of any use to me or to anyone else,' said Mehta Kalu.

'Stop it,' Rai Bular called, when he knew he was within hearing distance, his voice stern and authoritative. 'Stop it at once. Do you want to kill the boy with the weight of your reproach?'

'It would be a less painful closure for both him and me,' said Mehta Kalu.

'You only say that because you know my helplessness. As a Muslim, both society and custom forbid me to take him into my house, to do what I have always wanted to do – to adopt him as my son. Listen to me. Listen to what the boy has to say before you make up your mind and tell him that he is useless and that he is a failure,' said Rai Bular.

Mehta Kalu let his friend's words sink in and finally found control over his emotions.

Rai Bular continued speaking: 'You wanted him to make a true bargain. With your understanding and your beliefs, a true bargain in business would mean the gaining of a neat profit in terms of money – money that would be used to buy luxuries for yourself and your family. But look at it from Nanak's point of view. You have always known that he has been cast in a different mould from the rest of us. You know of his fixed and determined beliefs. You know that these beliefs often come into conflict with the beliefs that tradition imposes on us. He had his own understanding of what a true bargain would be. Being detached from the world and from material things, a true bargain for him was a bargain that was true in the eyes of God. So he used the money to feed a whole *akhara* of famished sadhus. Now in the eyes of God, what would be a truer bargain: a bargain that would earn you money for some additional luxuries or a bargain which ensured that a group of sadhus, a group of God's men, would not starve to death?'

There was no argument that Mehta Kalu could advance to counter what his friend had said, but neither did his friend's interpretation do very much to dissipate the strong sense of disappointment that he felt in his heart.

As for Nanak, nothing could shake his conviction that what he had done was the right thing. The song returned to his heart and there was once again a spring in his step. If he needed any further reassurance, it came from Rai Bular and from his own mother Tripta. They showered their love on him, lost no opportunity to tell him how proud they were of what he had done and repeated the story to anyone who cared to listen. Pandit Hardyal too, on his part, was extremely proud of his protégé and of what he had done. He repeated again and again that, when he had first cast Nanak's horoscope, he had seen strong signs of greatness in the infant's future. This prediction was now being borne out, not only in Nanak's prodigious ability to compose metaphysical, mystic verses but also in his conduct.

He would challenge his listeners by saying: 'Tell me. Do you know of any other sixteen-year-old who has shown such maturity and such kinship with God? Who other than Nanak would choose to feed the hungry sadhus rather than earn a profit for himself?'

In the months to come, even the most diehard critic of Nanak and those cynical towards him veered around to the view that what he had done was not only special and unique but also showed his deep understanding of God's ways. They all started to regard him with respect and awe and waited for the far greater things that lay ahead in the boy's future.

Let compassion be your mosque,
Devotion your prayer mat,
Truth and fairplay your Holy Qur'an,
Let your modesty be your circumcision,
And courtesy your fast.
Let your conduct be the Kaaba.
Rectitude your guide,
And good deeds your creed and prayer:
Thy rosary should be what pleases Him.
Thus would He safeguard your honour.[9]

– *Var Majh, Shlok 1, Pauri 7*

Chapter 3

The Guru and the Qazi

An uneasy calm prevailed in the Bedi household. Mehta Kalu had learnt to rein in his true feelings about his son Nanak's 'disastrous' business venture. He went about his work as usual and had a kind word and an affectionate greeting for all whom he met. His family, friends and acquaintances were convinced that he had taken the whole affair in his stride and had come to terms not only with his loss but also with the fact that his son was different from the other young men in Talwandi. But those who were close to him, including his wife Tripta and his employer Rai Bular, could not help but notice the diffidence in his manner, the slight restraint that had come between him and those around him. This was particularly true in his relationship with his son. He was polite towards the boy, but there was a holding back: a formality, an absence of any real warmth or affection in his interactions with him. The anger and frustration still stayed firmly in his heart. Nothing had helped to make them go away or to soften them, not even the passage of time.

Tripta's repeated reassurances that all would be well, that Nanak was an unworldly boy and it had been a mistake to expect him to be successful in a business venture, did little to help diffuse the situation at home. The Rai's repeated assertions that Mehta Kalu must look at the world from Nanak's point of view, that in the eyes of the wise and the saintly, his son had already achieved greatness – a greatness that they should understand and respect and admire – were listened to politely but seemed to have no lasting effect on Nanak's father. Both Tripta and the Rai knew that Mehta Kalu's hostility towards his son was deeply ensconced in his heart and waited – like a coiled serpent – for an opportunity to strike. They both worried about it.

Then a solution presented itself. Nanki, Nanak's sister, well aware of the situation in her father's home, discussed the matter with her husband Jai Ram. Nanki's husband was a revenue official in the employment of Nawab Daulat Khan Lodhi, the governor of Sultanpur. Jai Ram was extremely fond of his brother-in-law and, like Pandit Hardyal, recognized the seeds of greatness in the boy. He immediately suggested that they invite Nanak to Sultanpur and find him employment with the nawab. There would then be no danger of Mehta Kalu giving vent to his pent-up anger. Perhaps, seeing that Nanak was now 'gainfully' employed, he might eventually put the past experience behind, which may help open a new chapter in his relationship with his son.

Mehta Kalu discussed the offer with Tripta and Rai Bular, who strongly advised that the offer should be accepted.

Nanak moved to Sultanpur (around 60 km from Talwandi) where he found employment with Nawab Daulat Khan. Daulat Khan was so impressed with his cheerful nature, honesty and diligence that he soon appointed him as the keeper of his *modikhana* (store), a task which Nanak performed with utmost honesty and diligence. Soon Nanak's life had established its own rhythm: He would get up in the morning, go and bathe in the Bein rivulet, spend some time on its bank in prayer and meditation, come home and, after breakfast, go to the *modikhana* for the day's work. In the evenings, a small group of people would assemble in his house to listen to the hymns he had composed.

It was during this time that Nanak became a family man. He got married on 24 September 1487 to the gentle, kind-hearted Sulakhini, daughter of Mul Chand and Chando Rani of the town of Batala. Mul Chand belonged to the Chona subcaste of the Kshatriyas[10] and looked after the lands of the Randhawa Jats in the village of Pakhoke. Nanak was blessed with two sons, Sri Chand (8 September 1494) and Lakhmi Das (12 February 1497).

Professionally, Nanak was doing well and Daulat Khan lost no opportunity in showering praise on him and in showing him favours, which naturally led to jealousy among the other, more senior officials in the nawab's court. They soon started a vilification campaign and spread rumours about Nanak's integrity. Nanak too heard these rumours and insisted that an audit of the stores be conducted. Everything was found in order.

However, Nanak got mentally and emotionally disturbed.

One day, Nanak did not return from his bath in the stream. When the family went to look for him, they found his clothes on the river bank but there was no sign of him. So they concluded that perhaps he had drowned. The news spread and a worried Daulat Khan too rushed to the spot, his officers riding close behind him.

'Get the fishermen's net. Hurry ... send in the most experienced divers to search the river bed,' he shouted.

While his orders were being carried out his mind turned to Nanak. He knew that Nanak was a strong swimmer, so it was unlikely that he could have come to any harm in the rivulet. But then he remembered the recent happenings and how disturbed Nanak had been in spite of all his reassurances. Perhaps in this disturbed state of mind, he had been a little careless and swum into a part of the stream with a strong undercurrent and had been carried away. Hours passed and one by one his officers returned.

The Guru and the Qazi

'Did you find anything?' he asked and each of them shook his head in the negative. Daulat Khan still did not believe that the worst had happened and the one other person who shared his belief was Nanki, Nanak's sister.

'You wait and see,' she would say to all she met. 'My brother will return safe.'

A week later, Nanak indeed returned safe and sound. Daulat Khan's men found him wandering on the left bank of the river and brought him home. In answer to the queries that were addressed to him, he would only shake his head, give a radiant smile and declare: 'There is only one God. There is no Hindu, no Mussalman.'

This was to be his constant refrain over the next few days: 'There is no Hindu, there is no Mussalman.'

Many of those who heard him were convinced that Nanak had lost his sense of reasoning. His followers, however, would go on repeating their master's refrain: 'There is no Hindu, there is no Mussalman'. Soon, the chant could be heard everywhere. The devout Muslims were upset because they felt that Nanak was encouraging people to become heretics. The orthodox became exceedingly alarmed. They knew they needed to counter this growing heretic tendency, even among some of their own people. A delegation was sent to report the matter to the qazi* of Sultanpur.

The leader of the delegates spoke thus: 'Your holiness. This kafir is saying over and over again, "There is no Hindu,

---

*A judge well versed with Islamic law.

there is no Mussalman." Though we do not understand exactly what he means, we feel that he is denigrating Muslims and is undermining our faith, the faith of all Muslims.'

The qazi was already wary of Nanak and a little jealous, because the latter had won great respect and love among the residents of Sultanpur, both Hindus and Muslims, with his kind, gentle ways and his concern for the poor and the underprivileged. The qazi was also concerned that, with this new message, Nanak would wean Muslims away from the teachings of the Quran. He went immediately to see Nawab Daulat Khan.

'Lord, this man must be stopped immediately ...', the qazi began. Daulat Khan could see that he was extremely angry. 'He can say what he likes about the Hindus, but he has no business to say that there is no Mussalman,' ended the qazi.

Daulat Khan had come to love Nanak dearly and had been overjoyed when he had reappeared after his week-long vanishing act. But he had also heard of the strange words that Nanak was repeatedly saying to all who would listen to him that 'there is no Hindu or Mussalman'. Now that the qazi had come to him, he knew that something had to be done to stop Nanak before all the Muslims were aroused against him, which they would be if the qazi took matters into his own hands. Daulat Khan was a gentle, secular human being at heart and did not want a communal riot on his hands. He sent for Nanak.

'Tell us Nanak, what you mean when you say there is no Hindu, there is no Mussalman. Are not the qazi and I,

The Guru and the Qazi

as followers of the Prophet Muhammad – peace be upon his soul – true Muslims?' asked Daulat Khan.

'There is no Hindu, no Mussalman,' Nanak repeated again. 'There are only true followers of God. We must be firm in our faith, our hearts must be pure, and not harbour any greed and pride. We must be unselfish and our kindness must embrace all of mankind. Only then can we call ourselves true Hindus or true Mussalmans,' Nanak explained.

'And what are you?' The qazi's face was red with anger and his voice was shrill and loud as he voiced this question.

Nanak only smiled at this display of anger and, in his usual soft gentle voice, replied: 'I am neither a Hindu nor a Mussalman.'

'Why?' asked the qazi.

'That is because I believe in the teachings of all religions. To me the teachings of all religions lead to God,' responded Nanak.

The qazi thought he saw an opportunity to trap Nanak and expose him as a charlatan.

'The time has come for the Friday prayers. If you believe that all religions lead to God then you will have no objection to joining us in the namaz?' asked the qazi.

'I will do that with pleasure. I will follow when you lead the prayers,' said Nanak.

So the nawab, the qazi and Nanak set off for the mosque. The qazi took his place at the head of the congregation. During the namaz, while all the other worshippers knelt, Nanak remained standing. The qazi saw this and, as soon as the namaz was over, he turned to the nawab and said:

'See, my lord, this man is a liar and a cheat. He said that for him all religions are equal and he would join us in the namaz. But he did not do so. He must be punished for his lies and for his heretical teachings.' The nawab turned to Nanak, shocked at this turn of events.

'Tell me my friend what do you have to say about the qazi's accusation?' asked Daulat Khan.

Nanak did not reply to the nawab's question. He turned instead to the qazi. With a smile on his lips and a twinkle in his eyes, he said: 'You are a man of God in the house of God and you have just led a thousand men in prayer. We stand in a place that has been hallowed and made sacrosanct by the prayers of thousands of devout Muslims. I know you will tell the truth and only the truth. Tell me what was on your mind as you led the prayers?'

The qazi thought for a while and then he saw that the smile from Nanak's lips had spread to his entire face, a face that was diffused with gentleness and kindness that he had never seen before. He knew then that he must tell the truth to such a person.

'I was thinking of my mare and her foal,' the qazi spoke softly, but the silence around him was so complete that everyone could hear him.

'My mare gave birth to a foal last night. It was a difficult birthing but the foal is truly beautiful. They are both in a stable close to an open well and my thoughts kept going back to them while I prayed. I worried that the mare or the foal would fall into the well,' the qazi finished.

'So tell me O holy one, does prayer consist merely of

kneeling and bowing and reciting a few words? Did you really lead the prayers in the true sense of the word then?' asked Nanak.

'No,' the qazi said, at last understanding the import of what Nanak had been trying to say through his 'heretical' teaching.

'Prayer is a tool to control the mind so that when you raise your voice in prayer to God you think only of him and of nothing else. You are right Nanak; while my body was bowing and my voice was reciting the holy words, my mind did not dwell on God but on mundane matters .... My prayers were not true prayers and so I did not lead the prayers. I failed my God and my religion. I failed to be a true man of God and I failed to be a Mussalman,' the qazi accepted.

O Nanak, to usurp another's right is forbidden,
As is the flesh of swine to the Muslim
And the flesh of the cow to the Hindu.
Your Guru the mentor will stand by you
if you covet not another's goods
But reject it as carrion.

– *Majh di Var*[11]

Chapter 4

BHAI LALO

*A*FTER HIS ELIGHTENMENT IN THE RIVER, THE GROUP of people who collected in Nanak's house every evening to listen to his Bani[12] grew larger with each passing day till it became a sizeable gathering. They were, in every respect, his disciples and the most ardent of these disciples were his sister Nanki and her husband Jai Ram.

Nanak soon realized that the message he had to give to humanity needed to be spread beyond the confines of Sultanpur. Since his teachings were radical and often in conflict with some of the rites and rituals that were being practised at the time in the name of Hinduism and Islam, they would not find ready acceptance among people. He needed to meet them face to face to explain his thoughts for them to find acceptance. Since people living at a distance were not likely to come to him, there was only one way of getting his message across to them – he needed to go to them.

So Nanak dressed himself in a strange garb – an approximate combination of what the holy men of Hinduism and of Islam would wear – to emphasize the universality of his teachings. Accompanied by his friend

Mardana, the rabaab[13] player, Nanak set out on his travels which would take him to all the four corners of the country and to places that lay beyond India's then-known boundaries.

Accounts vary on the number of journeys that Guru Nanak undertook in order to spread his message of love, brotherhood and equality. According to the Puratan Janamsakhi, one of the oldest accounts of the life history of Guru Nanak, he undertook five journeys (also known as *udasis*) and travelled far and wide. These are:

First *udasi* (1499–1506):
It lasted about seven years and covered the following towns and regions: Sultanpur, Tulamba (modern Makhdumpur, in Multan, Pakistan), Panipat, Delhi, Benaras (Varanasi), Nanakmata (now known as Nainital, Uttaranchal), Tanda Vanjara (Rampur, Uttar Pradesh), Kamrup (Assam), Asa Desh (Assam), Saidpur, Pasrur and Sialkot (all three in Pakistan).

Second *udasi* (1506–1513):
It lasted about seven years and covered the following towns and regions: Dhanasri Valley (Assam) and Sangladip in Ceylon (now Sri Lanka).

Third *udasi* (1514–1518):
It lasted about four years and covered certain regions in Kashmir, Sumer Parbat (in the Himalayas), Nepal, Tashkent, Sikkim and Tibet.

Fourth *udasi* (1519–1521):
It lasted about two years and covered the regions near Mecca and the Arab countries.

Fifth *udasi* (1523–1524):
This lasted about one year and covered the towns and regions within Punjab.

However, more modern accounts point out that Guru Nanak undertook four travels, in the four cardinal directions of the compass, which spanned twenty-three years. Accordingly, these were:

First *udasi* (1499–1505): This was to the central and eastern parts of India.

Second *udasi* (1506–1509): This took him to important towns and religious centres of southern India and Sri Lanka.

Third *udasi* (1514–1516): This took him to the Gangetic plains as well as Bihar, Nepal, Lhasa, Leh, as far as Tashkent and then back to Punjab via the Kashmir Valley.

Fourth *udasi* (1518–1521): This took him to various Arab countries.

Personally, I believe that he undertook four *udasis* and not five.

The first was towards the east. From Sultanpur, Nanak went to Talwandi and spent some time with his parents from where he turned north-west towards the town of Saidpur.

It was that time of the day when the evening shadows lengthen and the day is finally ready to accept defeat in its valiant effort to keep the gathering darkness at bay. With the onset of dusk, there was a nip in the air. A breeze, sharp in its coldness, gathered strength and Nanak drew his chaddar close around his shoulders.

Nanak and Mardana were both weary and footsore from the long hours of walking and were relieved when they finally came within sight of their destination. Even in the gathering gloom they could see the walls of a *haveli* (mansion) towering over the rest of the village. Lamps were lit in quick succession in the habitation that they were now approaching. Mardana took a deep breath and smelt the smoke of a dozen cooking fires. This sharp, pungent smell served to sharpen his perpetual hunger to the point that he forgot all his weariness, and, quickening his step, hurried towards the village. Nanak smiled to himself and hurried after him.

Saidpur, like most villages of the time, centred around the *haveli* of the zamindar (landowner) or, if the zamindar lived elsewhere, the official who had been appointed by the zamindar as his revenue collector.

The official in this case was a middle-aged man named Malik Bhago Mal. His *haveli*, majestic and proud in all its splendour and beauty, stood in the centre of a vast compound. Though it was surrounded by a high wall to give the family privacy from the prying eyes of the other villagers, the wall did nothing to hide the beauty of the upper floors which could be seen and admired from a distance even by travellers approaching the village.

The *haveli* was surrounded in concentric circles by the houses of the other villagers, first by those belonging to the highest caste and then, in a progressively decreasing order of their positions in the village hierarchy, till finally, the very outskirts of the village were taken up by the homes of the lowest of the lower castes, the untouchables. The houses, in their design and construction, displayed the social status of their owners.

Those nearest to the *haveli* were grand two-storey structures of brick, which would have been impressive in their own right if they had not been overshadowed by the splendour of the *haveli*. These gave way to single storey brick houses which, in turn, were replaced by smaller mud houses, until, finally, one reached the single room, thatched shanties of the untouchables.

Nanak stopped at the door of the first shanty that they came to and knocked gently at the door. It was opened by a middle-aged, slightly built man. He held a little earthen oil lamp in his hands, which lit up the faces of his visitors. He stared curiously, first at Mardana and then at Nanak and, recognizing them as strangers, thought that they must have lost their way and had stopped to ask for directions. In deference to their higher social status, he took a step backwards, cast his eyes to the ground and in a voice that was little more than a whisper asked: 'Where do you wish to go, your honour? If it is the *haveli*, you only have to follow the path without taking any turn on the way and you will be at the gate. If it is somewhere else, please tell me and I will be only too glad to escort you there.'

Nanak put his hand on the speaker's shoulder and felt him wince under his touch.

'What is your name, my friend?' Nanak asked.

'People call me Lalo. I am a carpenter,' the man replied.

'Bhai Lalo, we are travellers and have walked a long way today. We are tired and weary and all that we wish for is a place to rest our weary limbs,' said Nanak.

'And a little food too in order to satisfy the hunger that gnaws at our stomachs,' Mardana added in a low voice, afraid that the promise that those cooking fires had held out to him would be belied. He saw no fire in the little courtyard, no welcome smell of freshly cooked food.

'I will escort you to the *dharamshala* – an inn for travellers. You will find comfortable lodgings there. I have heard they have a very good cook,' said the man.

Nanak looked around the little compound and said, 'Not as comfortable as your home would be, my friend.'

Nanak saw the shock in Lalo's eyes and was amused. He had been through this situation so often before, seen that look of shock again and again.

'No,' Lalo said, incredulously, as he stepped further back. His body seemed to have shrunk further into itself, as if he wanted to minimize his existence as much as he could. 'No, your honour, you cannot stay here. I belong to a low caste. You cannot stay with me. You would lose face in your community. You might even be excommunicated from your *biradari* [community],' Lalo added.

Once again Nanak put his arm around Lalo's shoulders and assured him: 'Don't worry, my friend. I have lost face and been threatened with excommunication by my *biradiri* so often before, that it no longer bothers me. As I said, I would be more comfortable here in your home with you than I would be in the *dharamshala*.' He paused for breath and, as Lalo looked up into his face, he saw an unmistakable twinkle come into his eye and when he spoke again there was laughter in his voice: 'Unless of course, you do not want us here.'

'No, no my lord,' Lalo held up his hands, palms facing Nanak and shook them from side to side. They had become an extension of his voice, embellishing his words. 'I am deeply honoured that you have chosen my home for your rest. It is only that the very limited hospitality that I have to offer does not befit your high status,' Lalo added.

Nanak took Lalo's hands in his and looking into his eyes said in the gentlest of tones, 'It is we who are honoured Bhai Lalo to be the recipients of your hospitality, to be guests in your home. Remember, in God's eyes a man's worth is never measured in terms of his caste or social status or his wealth. It is measured only by the nature of his deeds.'

Lalo led them through the postage stamp-sized courtyard into a little room and Nanak saw, towards one side of this courtyard, two low walled enclosures, one with a little brick hearth and a few utensils placed carefully on the wall and the other with two buckets standing side by side. And all the while, the only source of illumination was the little oil lamp that he carried in his hand. Nanak realized that Lalo had no other lamp, that he couldn't afford another lamp. The only furniture in the room, if it could be dignified by that name, was a loosely strung *charpoy* (a four-legged bed) on which he invited his guests to take rest. He placed the oil lamp in a little alcove in the wall and Nanak noticed the two or three articles of threadbare clothing that hung from a nail in the wall close to the alcove. He looked around the room. There was nothing else in it.

Their host left the room only to return a moment later with a mug of water.

'I am afraid the water is not warm. If I had known of your coming, I would have lit a fire and warmed it for you,' said Lalo. He knelt on the ground and washed first Nanak's feet and then Mardana's, and watching him at this task, Nanak knew that he lit a fire only once a day and cooked both his meals on that one fire, eating a cold evening meal.

'Don't bother to warm our food for us,' he said. 'My friend Mardana is so hungry that he would probably die of hunger before you could get the fire going.'

Lalo went out again and returned soon enough with a plate that had seen better days. On the plate lay a single, thick *bajre ki roti* (millet roti) and a single, small onion.

Mardana took one look at the thali and declared: 'I am not hungry, master.'

It was all that he could do to keep the disgust out of his voice. If Lalo noticed the contradiction between what the master had just said and Mardana's reaction to the food, he did not comment upon it. Remembering the sudden spurt of speed that Mardana had put on in the last lap of their journey a short while ago, Nanak knew why he was turning away from the food. He broke the roti into three portions.

'Don't look on this bread as food, look upon it as *prasad* (devotional offering),' Nanak said.

'I have eaten already my lord,' Lalo said, attempting to decline Nanak's offer of one-third of a roti.

'I know. As I said, look on this as *prasad*,' Nanak repeated, smiling at the thought that their host would probably steal quietly into the courtyard later to satisfy his hunger with a jug of water.

So, the three of them sat in the dim light of the little oil lamp, chewing on their portions of the single roti and their slivers of onion.

The spartan meal was soon over and preparations were made to go to bed. Nanak and Mardana shared the *charpoy*, covering themselves with the thin, threadbare quilt that Lalo brought out from a battered wooden box under the *charpoy*.

Lalo himself spread a single chaddar, as worn-out as the quilt on the floor and curling himself up against the cold, exhausted by the day's labour, drifted off to sleep, weary and content at the same time.

The lamp burnt itself out and later, much later, when both Mardana and Lalo were fast asleep, Nanak stole from the *charpoy* and covered Lalo with his own chaddar, knowing that it would give him some respite from the cold of the night.

Nanak awoke next morning to the sound of the soft melodious singing of a Kabir[14] bhajan. He continued to lie on the *charpoy* for a little longer, listening to his host singing as he went about the task of sweeping his little courtyard. He was touched by Lalo's melodious voice but moved even more by the deep contentment that each note exuded.

Then Nanak rose from the cot and went out into the courtyard to join his host. The moment he saw him, Lalo called out a cheerful greeting and, abandoning his work, ran to touch the Guru's feet. Nanak put his hand on his head in blessing.

'You're up early my friend,' Nanak said lightly and Lalo had indeed been up for some time now. He had hot water ready for Nanak and Mardana's bath and, by the time they had finished their ablutions and said their prayers, he had their morning meal ready for them.

While they ate, Lalo looked steadily into Nanak's eyes and the latter asked: 'There is something on your mind. What is it my friend?'

'I have a favour to ask. But I do not know if you will grant it,' answered Lalo.

'If it is within my power to grant it you know that I will,' said Nanak.

Lalo cleared his throat and said: 'You have done great honour to me and brought me great joy and blessing by gracing my little hut with your presence. I would wish for you to stay with me for a few days so that I can bask in the glory of your presence.'

All the time he spoke, his eyes were fixed on Nanak's

face. He did not even permit himself to blink for fear that he would miss an expression on that radiant face.

'You are being fulsome in your praise and in your gratitude. Why? You do not even know who I am,' said Nanak.

'I know that you are a man of God and that is enough for me. The fact that a man of God has chosen to grace my home means that God is pleased with me. I would wish to savour this pleasure a little longer,' said Lalo.

'You too Bhai Lalo are a man of God and I can assure you that you do not need my presence to tell you that God is pleased with you. But yes, if it means so much to you, I will stay with you a little longer,' Nanak said. He paused for a moment and then went on: 'But my acceding to your request comes with a rider: you will not treat me as a guest and do no more for me than what you do for yourself in attending to our needs.' He saw the dismay in Lalo's eyes but still continued speaking: 'If you cannot assure me of this, I must be on my way.'

He made as if to get up and Lalo cried out in despair: 'No my lord, do not go. I promise to do anything that you ask of me.'

Nanak settled down again, glad that his little ruse had worked so well. 'Now go to work and don't worry about us. There's much that we need to do,' said Nanak.

Lalo hurried out to the site where Ramdev, the master carpenter, had engaged him on a daily wage, marvelling at the prescience displayed by Nanak. He lived such a hand-to-mouth existence that he could not afford to miss a single day of work; if he did, he would starve.

Nanak and Mardana settled down to their morning prayers at the end of which, with Mardana playing the rabaab, Nanak sang one of his early compositions. The neighbours on hearing the singing were consumed by curiosity and crowded at the door, peering in to see who was responsible for such sweet and wonderful music. When Nanak, seeing them standing there, signalled to them to come in, they stole into the courtyard and sat down on the bare floor. Nobody could take their attention off the words of Nanak's song *Ik Onkar Satnam* ... (there is only one God Satnam ...) a song they had never heard before.

Word soon spread through the village, and people came to see the holy man who had camped in Lalo's hut. Nanak welcomed them with kind words and a smile on his face. They soon found themselves being drawn towards the stranger and towards the new way of life that he preached through his Bani.

When Lalo returned home that evening, it was to see a crowd of villagers listening with rapt attention to Nanak's words and when he said gently: 'It is time now for prayer,' they lapsed into pin drop silence. Mardana struck the first notes on his rabaab and Nanak began a recitation-cum-singing of his Bani. Lalo knew that the group of listeners hung with breathless, rapt attention onto every word that Nanak sang. Lalo stole quietly into the courtyard and joined the crowd. But if he thought that his arrival had gone unnoticed, he was mistaken because, as soon as Nanak finished his Bani, he said: 'Bhai Lalo will now lead us in the singing of one of Bhagat Kabir's hymns. Come Bhai Lalo, come and sit here so that we can all hear you.'

Mardana and Lalo exchanged a few words so that Mardana could get the accompaniment right on his rabaab.

Then Lalo began to sing. The song began as a hesitant, wavering melody but soon soared into its full strength. Because it was a well-known and well-loved song, the words were familiar to everyone in the gathering and soon the singing became a full-throated, beautiful chorus rendering. People were drawn even more to Nanak by the fact that he was open to all shades of religious beliefs.

Malik Bhago Mal, the revenue collector for the zamindar, was an exceedingly rich man who made sure that the tenant farmers and those who laboured for him in his household had enough to eat to keep their body and soul together. Other than this, he made sure that they had nothing more. The *lagaan* (land tax) had been fixed by the landlord many years ago and he had added his own percentage of commission to it. This percentage increased by leaps and bounds over the years, in proportion to the increase in his greed. The zamindar, as long as he got his *lagaan* regularly, was not concerned with anything else.

He made no concessions when there was a drought or a flood or the crop was ruined, running up the *lagaan* that was due, as a debit figure in the accounts of each of them, to be paid out of their share in the years when the harvest was plentiful. Through his *munshi* or accountant, who was the keeper of all his records and accounts, he also functioned as a proxy moneylender. The tenant farmers or the labourers, when they came face to face with a marriage or a death in the family, found they had no money for the expensive rituals that they were enjoined upon to perform on the occasion. In their despair they turned to the *munshi* who would give them loans at such usurious rates of interest that he ensured that never again would they be free from the debt that they had called upon themselves. They would have to remain, for the rest of their lives, bonded slaves to Malik Bhago and often their children, after them, would have to remain in slavery too because of their fathers' debts.

In spite of his cruelty and greed and his ruthless exploitation of the poor, Malik Bhago was sure that he would, after his death, find a place in heaven. This conviction came from certain practices that he followed religiously in his life. He had built a little temple in the courtyard of his *haveli* and had hired a group of priests to pray constantly for his well-being in this world and in the next. The priests prayed in a relay and the prayers never ceased. Bhago himself was too busy in his various ventures to participate in these prayers, but he did put in a cursory appearance when he had visitors whom he wanted to impress with his piety.

Twice a year, on his own birthday and on that of his only son, he hosted a grand feast for all the poor and impoverished people of the area. These were rich feasts with all kinds of delicacies being served, delicacies that the guests could only dream of during the rest of the year. He had dozens of cooks working round the clock to feed the hordes of the poor who descended on the *haveli* on these occasions. The feast started from early morning and ended only when the last hungry guest had been fed. Malik Bhago put in an appearance from time to time and found real satisfaction in seeing the large number of people he was feeding. He knew that they would all go home with deep gratitude in their hearts and, in their prayers, they would pray for the man who had fed them in such a generous and lavish manner. And hearing these prayers, God would be moved to give him a place at His feet, when his time came to ascend to the other world.

On the seventh day of the Navratras – a festival dedicated to the worship of the Hindu Goddess Durga – with unfailing regularity, he would organize an even richer and grander feast for all the religious men in the region. Days before the auspicious occasion, his emissaries would go forth and travel from village to village reminding all the swamis, the sadhus and the *bairagis (*devotional singers) of the approach of the auspicious day and of the impending feast. As with the poor, Malik Bhago was certain that the holy men who came and partook of the feast would all go back with gratitude in their hearts and prayers for the well-being of their host. He was certain that God would not be able to turn a deaf ear to the prayers of these highly evolved souls.

Because he was feeding holy men, he made sure that all his cooks and those who served the food were Brahmins – the highest of the four Hindu castes. No person, man or woman, belonging to a lower caste was permitted in the vicinity of the *haveli* on these days. Malik Bhago himself would put in a brief appearance once or twice during the day. He would look around, smile indulgently at his guests and then disappear into the interiors of the *haveli*. There were many among the crowd of holy men who were angered by the arrogance that he displayed and by the patronizing attitude that his body language indicated. Left to themselves, they would rather not have come. But then Malik Bhago was a powerful man and it would never do, even for a holy man, to anger him. So, in spite of the anger that so many of them nursed in their hearts, they all came.

It so happened that in that particular year, the Navratras occurred during Nanak's sojourn in Saidpur. By now, his presence had drawn so much attention that it could not but be noticed by both Malik Bhago and his emissaries and a special invitation was sent to him for the feast.

From the conversations of the people who flocked daily to his prayer meetings and those who came to him for advice, Nanak had a fair idea of the kind of person that Malik Bhago was. He did not go to the feast. During the afternoon, one of Malik Bhago's men noticed that Nanak had not joined the feast. He told Malik Bhago of this and a second invitation was dispatched. Nanak still did not go. In the evening, when the last group of holy men were being fed and Malik Bhago looked at them with deep satisfaction, he turned to his *munshi* and asked: 'Have all the holy men of the region been fed, all the sants, swamis, sadhus and ascetics?'

It was a rhetorical question and he expected only yes as an answer. However, he was greatly surprised when the *munshi* replied: 'All your honour, except the one who calls himself Nanak, the one who has camped in Lalo's hut, and Mardana.'

'Was he not informed about the feast?' asked Malik Bhago.

'Yes he was, not once but twice,' replied the *munshi*.

'Twice? And yet he did not come?' Malik Bhago's face turned red with anger as he said this. How dare this wandering sadhu refuse his, Malik Bhago's, invitation he thought to himself! He controlled his anger and said mildly: 'Go to him again. Tell him that I will not insist if he does not desire to partake of my feast. But I would like him to come, would like more than anything to exchange a few words with him.'

The emissary arrived at Lalo's hut and conveyed Malik Bhago's message to Nanak. Nanak knew that he had hurt the landlord's ego and that he was angry beyond words. He also knew that if he did not go, poor Lalo would have to bear the brunt of Malik Bhago's ire. So calling out to Mardana to accompany him, he made his way to the *haveli*.

Word had got around about the impending confrontation. Some of the sadhus who had still been in the vicinity of the *haveli* had returned to see how the situation would play out. The villagers, even those belonging to the lower castes, forgetting Malik Bhago's injunction for the day, crowded into the vast courtyard. The emissary went in to inform Malik Bhago of Nanak's arrival as a hushed silence descended on the crowd.

Nanak, through his gentle and endearing nature and through his prayer meetings, had made a profound impression upon the villagers. Yet, so great was the fear of what Malik Bhago could do to them that not one crossed over to where Nanak and Mardana stood. At last, Malik Bhago appeared at the door. The crowd bowed to him and Nanak folded his hands and held them up in greeting.

'So you are the great Nanak, who feels it is below his dignity to accept Malik Bhago's invitation to his feast!' said Malik Bhago.

Though Nanak looked back into those dark angry eyes without flinching, he did not say anything.

'Lay on the feast,' Malik Bhago called to one of the attendants. Portions of all the twenty-one dishes that had been cooked were laid out for Nanak.

'Look Nanak, look. Look at the richness of the food that I have prepared for you. It contains the best delicacies that money can buy. I am sure that you have never in your life seen or eaten such satisfying and delicious food,' said Malik Bhago.

Nanak smiled at this display of overweening arrogance and pride and said: 'I have tasted much richer and more delicious food than this.'

There were many who trembled for him and for the stand that he had taken against Malik Bhago.

'You have? Where?' Bhago asked incredulously.

Nanak asked Mardana to hurry back to Lalo's hut and bring some portion of what was to be their evening meal.

BHAI LALO

Mardana returned soon enough with a thick roti made of coarse *bajra*. This Nanak held up for Malik Bhago to see. The crowd sent up a collective gasp of surprise and Malik Bhago burst into loud laughter. When he had finally exhausted his amusement, he turned to Nanak and asked: 'What kind of joke is this? You find the coarse *bajre ki roti* from a wretched carpenter's hovel richer and tastier than all the food that lies at your feet? How do you expect anyone to believe this?'

To this Nanak replied: 'It is not a joke Malik Bhago, it is the truth. Look closely at the twenty-one dishes you have laid out for me and for all the other holy men. Where did the wherewithal for these dishes come from? You earned the means to be able to organize this feast by exploiting the poor. You keep them in such a state of penury that their lives are full of continual misery, an ongoing saga of suffering. The ingredients of your food are not the expensive spices and dry fruits and pure ghee that have gone into their making, they are the sweat and blood and tears of the suffering poor whom you have exploited so ruthlessly. You have hired priests to pray for you, but you yourself spend no time in remembering or thinking of God. Though you have so much in terms of material wealth, you are not content. You never thank God for what you have. Instead, all your thoughts and your energy are spent in getting more and more. You hold feasts for the poor and for the holy only to earn merit in the eyes of God, in the hope that they will all pray for you and that God will forgive you all your sins. When you organize these feasts it entails no sacrifice on your part.'

Nanak continued speaking: 'Lalo, on the other hand, prays regularly and thanks God with his every breath for whatever little has been given to him. Whatever he eats has been earned through hard labour with the sweat of his brow. When the need arises, he is prepared to go hungry so another can be fed and he makes this sacrifice willingly and cheerfully, with no hope or desire of earning anything from it. The ingredients of what you call his poor man's food are the milk of human kindness and generosity. How can the food that has been made with the blood and sweat and tears of the poor be in anyway richer and more delicious than the food that is made with the milk of human kindness?'

Malik Bhago was silent for a while, letting the import of Nanak's words sink in. Silent too was the crowd, marvelling at the fact that the truth had at last been brought out into the open. It went to Malik Bhago's credit that, face to face with Nanak, having listened to those telling words, his arrogance and pride fell away from him immediately. He fell to his knees at Nanak's feet, and burying his face in Nanak's robe, said: 'How true your words are O master and how mistaken I have been. Forgive me; I will do whatever is in my power to make amends for my actions and my conduct in the past.'

'It is not I who must forgive you. It is the people who have suffered at your hands who must forgive you. Live up to your promise. Make amends to such an extent that they cannot help but forgive you. Once they have forgiven you, God too will forgive you and you will find his grace,' Nanak declared.

Nanak moved on from Saidpur and, in the days and years that followed, Malik Bhago lived up to his promise to Nanak. A fresh and happy chapter, unclouded by exploitation, suffering and misery, opened up in the lives of the residents of Saidpur.

If one possessed the eighteen Puranas
And could recite the four Vedas by heart,
If one made pilgrimages to bathe on holy festivals
And gave alms in accord to one's caste,
If one fasted and performed the prescribed ceremonies,
Or became one a Qazi, a Mullah, or a Shaikh
A yogi, or a Jangam, in ochre dress,
Or a householder precise in religious ritual –
Without realization, all will be taken away in bondage.
By our acts we shall be judged.

Raag Basant[15]

Chapter 5

HARIDWAR AND GANGA

THE ICE THAT MELTS FROM THE MOUTH OF THE GLACIER at Gomukh[16] begins as a trickle, but, by the time it reaches Gangotri, it is a full-fledged mountain stream, rushing and gushing down the steep slopes of the Himalayas, tumbling down the narrow passage that it has carved for itself in the stony slopes. Here at Gangotri it is given the name of Bhagirathi. Legend has it that King Bhagirath brought this river down to earth through his prayers and meditation for the salvation of his ancestors, who had been cursed by the sage Kapil. It is as Bhagirathi that it flows all the way down to Devprayag, in Uttarakhand, where it is joined by the equally powerful and turbulent Alakananda. The river that results from this confluence is the Ganga, the holiest of the holy rivers of the Hindus.

From Devprayag, Ganga makes its playful journey down to Rishikesh where it breaks free of the Himalayas and wends its way through the Doon Valley in the Shivaliks. It is calmer now and more sedate in its movement, but the sound of its gushing water remains strong and it is clear that it is still very much a river of the mountains. It is only when it reaches the mouth of the valley and breaks free of the Shivaliks to enter the plains at Haridwar that it becomes a full-fledged river of the plains, its flow now bearing a stateliness and dignity it did not have before.

Haridwar is arguably the holiest of the many holy cities situated along the banks of this sacred river. The *char dham yatra* – the four abodes pilgrimage – begins from here and since there is a belief that whoever completes this yatra has found God, the name Haridwar or 'gateway to God' is most apt. After the *samudra manthan* (churning of the seas), when the celestial bird Garuda was carrying away the *amrit* (elixir of immortality) to keep it safe from the *Asuras* (a group of power-seeking demons) one of the four spots where drops fell was Haridwar. As a result, it has become one of the four important places of pilgrimage where the Kumbh Mela – believed to be the largest peaceful gathering on earth attended by around 100 million people – is held, every twelve years.

Another dimension is added to the sanctity and sacredness of Haridwar by the fact that almost all devout Hindus bring the last remains of their loved ones here and cast them in the waters of the Ganga in the hope that the dead will find salvation through this act. One of the rituals connected with worship at Haridwar is the offering of the sacred waters by the pilgrims to the spirit of their ancestors so that they too can achieve salvation like the ancestors of Bhagirath did when this sacred river was first brought down to Earth.

The exact spot where the *amrit* is said to have fallen in Haridwar, is called the Brahma Kund, which is located on the Har ki Pauri (steps of God), consequently considered to be the most holy of the ghats.

Nanak, having set out on the first of his four *udasis*, found himself in Haridwar the day before Baisakhi – the harvest festival celebrated annually on 13 April every year – in 1504.

Baisakhi, which also marks the beginning of the Hindu solar year, is celebrated throughout India in different ways and under different names. Its origins as a festival are primeval and go back to the time when human beings began to grow food instead of merely hunting for it. It marks the completion of the harvest and, in a primarily agrarian country like India, it is celebrated with joy and fervour as an occasion to thank God for his bounty in giving a plentiful harvest and to pray for future prosperity. As such, the joy and happiness that Baisakhi brings with it, cut across lines of religion and caste.

For the Buddhists, it commemorates the birth, the enlightenment and the death of the Buddha. The Hindus use the occasion of Baisakhi to celebrate the descent of the Goddess Ganga to earth thousands of years ago. In her honour millions of devout Hindus gather along the sacred river for ritual baths, with Haridwar being one of the most favoured spots.

When Nanak reached Haridwar the town was overcrowded with pilgrims. There was no accommodation to be had. After wandering around the streets for some length of time and failing to find even the barest and humblest of accommodation, Nanak and Mardana met a kindly swami – who recognizing the godliness in this strangely dressed pilgrim – took them to his ashram and made place for them in the already overcrowded premises.

The next morning the swami, knowing Nanak to be a man of God who would like to participate in the holy rituals, woke him up early and the two went swiftly through the early dawn to Har ki Pauri so as to be able to find a suitable place where they could perform the bathing ritual.

At last the sun broke over the horizon and the auspicious time had arrived. Nanak stood patiently looking at the people around him. He saw each of them take a dip in the holy river and then offering palmfuls of water to the sun and chanting mantras while doing it. The gesture was repeated again and again. Nanak knew the significance of this ritual and yet he waited for the swami to finish and asked: 'Do you offer the water to the Sun God?'

The swami smiled and answered: 'In a way you could say that. But the absolute truth is that we offer the water to our ancestors who now live in Suryalok or heaven, from where the Sun rises and where it descends in the evening. Since the only intermediary with heaven, which can indicate to us the right direction is the Sun, we offer the water to the rising Sun.'

'And what will the offering of the water do for your ancestors?' asked Nanak.

'It will bring them salvation like the coming of Mother

Ganga to earth brought salvation to the ancestors of King Bhagirath,' replied the swami.

Nanak was quiet for a while and the swami thought he was musing over what he had just been told. By now the first flush of the crowd on the ghats had begun to thin and there was plenty of space. 'Come holy one, the auspicious period of time is about to end. Make your offering and bring salvation to the souls of your ancestors,' the swami said to Nanak.

Nanak descended into the river and, after taking three dips in the holy waters, turned westwards, his back turned resolutely towards the rising Sun. He then began to make the offering of water the way he had seen the swami and the other pilgrims do. The swami stood by in silent amazement and gradually, as Nanak repeated the ritual over and over again, more and more pilgrims stopped in their tracks to watch this strange performance. At last the swami put a restraining hand on Nanak's arm and Nanak paused and looked at the swami. The swami smiled gently and said: 'You are facing in the wrong direction. You should be facing the Sun for your offering to reach your ancestors.'

'But I am not making an offering to my ancestors,' pointed out Nanak.

'If you are not making the offering to your ancestors then whom are you making it to?' the swami asked.

'I am making the offering to my land back home and that is why I am facing west, in the direction of Punjab. I am offering water to my newly ploughed fields there. I am sure my offering of water will benefit the next crop when it is sown shortly,' explained Nanak.

The crowd of pilgrims that had collected around them burst into laughter and those who had not been close enough to hear Nanak turned to their neighbours to find out what the strange man had said. They all shook their heads at Nanak's stupidity. Even the swami, with all his respect for Nanak's godliness, could not help but smile. He put his hand on Nanak's shoulders and very patiently, almost as if he was talking to a little child, said: 'Punjab is very far away and your offering of water will not reach that far.'

'You were offering water to your ancestors, who you said were now in heaven. How far is heaven from Haridwar?' asked Nanak.

The swami pondered over this question, wondering where the conversation was going and then replied: 'Heaven is forty-nine-and-a-half-crore *kos* [one *kos* is equivalent to about 3 km] away.'

Nanak smiled at the swami and said: 'If you are sure that your offering of water will reach heaven, which is forty-nine-and-a-half-crore *kos* away, then I can be very sure that my offering of water will reach my fields near Lahore, which are only a few hundred *kos* away.'

The people who had gathered around stared at Nanak in awe and amazement. The logic of what he had said was irrefutable. If the offerings of water could not reach Punjab, how could they then reach heaven, which was so much further away? It was an empty ritual that they had been performing all these years.

People, however, did not stop performing this ritual; in fact, more people perform it today than ever before.

However, there were a few present at the ghat that day who began to question the validity of this ritual, and by dwelling on its emptiness, they began to question the other rituals, which had become an integral part of their lives. Some of them desired to listen further to the words of this wise man and, in the evening, when Nanak held his usual satsang (an assembly for a spiritual discourse) in the ashram, they went and listened to his Bani in rapt attention.

The swami, of course, was profoundly influenced by Nanak's simple message and when, a few days later, it was time for Nanak to resume his journey eastwards, he walked with him and Mardana a good distance. When it was finally time to part, he touched Nanak's feet in recognition of his superior wisdom and, when he turned back towards Haridwar, there were tears in his eyes and a deep sense of loss in his heart. His sermons from then on were peppered with Nanak's thoughts. And those who had been impressed by Nanak's logic and the messages that he preached, returned to their villages and spread the word about the holy man and what he was attempting to teach: authenticity in behaviour and love towards another human being.

Nanak had touched the lives of many and the dissemination of the seeds of a new faith had begun.

Man is engrossed in the taste of gold, silver, woman,
fragrant substances, horses, soft beds, mansions,
sweet-tasting meals, flesh, food:
With all these tastes engrossing the body, how may
the Name find a lodging therein?
Nothing beyond this may be said: Those pleasing
God alone are good.
Such alone have wisdom, honour and true wealth,
As in their heart have Him lodged.

– *Raag Sri*[17]

Chapter 6

THE TWO SHOPKEEPERS

According to a scholar on Sikhism: 'He shared the hospitality of humble homes and he rested sometimes under the sky. He went to small unknown villages and he visited the seats of the mighty as well. He mixed with simple unlettered men and he discoursed with the learned. He attended fairs and festivals, and visited temples and mosques, hermitages and *khanaqahs* [meeting places of Sufis]. He spoke with individuals engaged in their daily trades and he preached to multitudes conveniently.... Many found peace in his gentle words of love and faith and were won over by his simple teaching.'[18]

Nanak and Mardana had still not got used to walking for hours on end and were perpetually suffering from foot sores. To add to their troubles, the monsoons had set in and it made the slushy terrain difficult and tiring to traverse. The rain would come in sudden and strong onslaughts, lashing their bodies, while the gusty winds threatened to tear the clothes off their backs. Things were made more difficult by the hordes of mosquitoes and other insects that descended on them, making their journey one long stretch of misery. Then there was also the humidity to deal with, which not only made them sweat profusely but also left them dehydrated and exhausted. Moreover, there were no well-defined roads in the area that they were traversing and, very often, after a particularly heavy and extended rainfall, they would find their legs sinking nearly up to their knees in the slush, making each step painful and laborious. And yet they trudged on as best as they could. They were weary and exhausted and close to the limit of their endurance and at the edge of their threshold of pain.

They came to a town, where everything spoke to them of prosperity and well-being. Though the town had grown in recent years, it was still not big enough to be called a city. The people were industrious and cheerful and God-fearing. Nanak decided that this would be the ideal place for them to make a pause in their journey. After a couple of weeks, the fury of the monsoon would have abated and it would be easier and more comfortable for them to go on.

He expressed his desire to stop here for a few days, perhaps a few weeks, and the people of the town welcomed him with open arms. They found comfortable accommodation for him and Mardana and attended to their every need. Nanak resumed his practice of singing his Bani every morning and evening when the weather permitted it. People came to attend these prayer meetings and to listen to the new way of life that he preached. They came, first in ones and twos and then, as word spread of his wonderful Bani and how easy he made the practice of the new religion seem, they came in hordes. His hosts had to find another, bigger venue for him to hold his prayer meetings. Nanak's reputation as a wise and learned man spread beyond the town and people from the neighbouring towns and villages also came to listen and to participate in the *kirtans* (religious singing). Soon, Nanak had garnered a huge following of disciples for his new religious philosophy.

One such family was of a small-time trader, who had done well with his small all-goods shop and was now looking to spread his wings and open a bigger establishment in a nearby town. He had heard the excited conversations in his family regarding the holy man and had been curious to know more about him.

One day, he went early in the morning to see a plot that was being offered to him. As he walked through the quiet streets of the town, he heard, first softly in the distance and then resonating louder and louder as he walked towards it, a voice raised in the singing of a prayer. It was a deep, mellifluous voice and the enunciation of the prayer was slow and clear. He could hear clearly each syllable, each word of the hymn.

He stopped in his tracks, mesmerized by the beauty of what he had heard, both in the voice and in the words. Then, as if drawn by a magic spell, he hurried towards the sound. He took off his shoes and joined the congregation, and, as he listened to the holy man expounding on the prayer that he had just sung, all doubts and anxieties fell away from him. Like the other members of his family, he too became a devout follower of Nanak and tried to practise everything that he preached. In the days that followed, attending the prayer meetings became a regular part of his daily routine. He listened to those words, sheer magic in their simplicity, and as he did so, he felt a deep stillness pervade every fibre of his body, every nook and corner of his soul. He had found the very centre of his being.

His family marvelled at the change they found in him. No longer was he in a hurry to get to his shop in the morning; no longer did he wish to be left strictly alone in the evening to write up his accounts. No longer was he angry with the children if they made too much noise while at play. He, who had been singularly devoid of a sense of humour, now found himself laughing with the children at their little harmless pranks and, wonder of wonders, he also said and did things that made other people laugh. Where before his manner towards other people had been marked by brusqueness that bordered on the rude, he now greeted each person he met with a broad open smile on his face and an easy, cordial manner as if he had all the time in the world for them.

His obsession with earning more and more also seemed to have waned quietly into some dark recess of his being. Instead, there was a warm feeling of contentment and satisfaction that radiated from his words and actions. His new obsession, his passion now – if something so serene and calm can be given these names – was the desire not to miss a single prayer meeting, to never lose his temper, to make an honest living even as a tradesman and to help

The Two Shopkeepers

those in need. He was now constantly reciting God's name and would break into one of Nanak's hymns spontaneously. This change in him was so great that it could not possibly escape the notice of anyone who came into contact with him now and who had known him earlier.

The neighbouring shop was owned by a handsome young man who was happy, cheerful and industrious in his own way. His attitude to life was in sheer contrast to that of the first shopkeeper. He was in business with the sole intent and purpose of making as much money as he could and had no compunction in exploiting his customers to the hilt. With his ill-gotten wealth, he gave himself up entirely to earthly pleasures. His philosophy in life was simple and hedonistic: In spite of what the holy men and the holy books say about birth, death and rebirth, this is the only life that we are certain of and life has many pleasures to offer that we should savour to the fullest.

Though there was a great difference in their individual attitudes to life, the two shopkeepers shared a friendly, cordial relationship.

One morning, the first shopkeeper was singing one of Nanak's hymns as he was opening his shop. The second shopkeeper, who had already opened his shop came out to greet his friend and heard the hymn. He did not catch the words but the melody appealed to him.

'What is this beautiful melody that you are singing?'

'It is a hymn composed by my Guru; his name is Nanak.'

'A hymn? How boring!' said the second shopkeeper, crinkling up his nose in disgust. He continued: 'Hymns are for the old and for those weary of the world. What business can young people have with matters pertaining to religion when there is so much else to occupy our hearts and our minds? There will be time enough for religion later.'

'There is time enough even now. If you will but come and listen to my Guru once, I promise it will change your life forever,' said Nanak's disciple.

'I am quite happy with my life as it is and do not wish to change it. But I am intrigued by the phenomenal change that has been wrought in you of late, and I would like to meet the man responsible for it,' said the other shopkeeper.

So it was decided that he would accompany the first shopkeeper to Nanak's satsang that evening. But he was not to attain a state of grace just yet. As they were walking together through the crowded streets that evening, the second shopkeeper caught the eye of a pretty young woman sitting on a first floor balcony. Immediately attracted, he stopped to smile at her. His companion saw the woman smile back and the silent signal that passed between the two. The second shopkeeper gave a short laugh, turned to him and slapping him on his back said: 'A greater bliss awaits me on that balcony. Your Guru will have to wait.'

'Adultery is a sin. By indulging in the pleasures of the moment do not condemn your soul to eternal damnation,' warned the disciple shopkeeper.

'What do I care for what happens to my soul? I'll be dead and gone and the dead feel nothing. For me the present is enough; it is all that matters,' retorted the second shopkeeper. He looked at his friend and gave a sly, wicked smile and, lowering his voice to an urgent whisper, said: 'Come with me my friend and taste the forbidden pleasure that you so strongly condemn. I assure you, you will forget the bliss that your Guru and his teachings bring you, by attaining a higher bliss. Like me, you too will stop giving a thought to sin and eternal damnation of the soul.'

The first shopkeeper shook his head sadly and remarked: 'You know not what you do. There can be no bliss greater than being a disciple of my Guru.'

'To each his own. You go to your bliss and I will go to mine,' the second shopkeeper said with a shrug of his shoulders.

The next morning, the first shopkeeper was singing his hymn with that same radiant smile on his face. The second shopkeeper realized that his friend's state of bliss was permanent while his own had lasted only till the satiation of his lust and thus was temporary. His curiosity was aroused again and he wanted to visit the Guru to find out what inspired that divine and perpetual state of happiness.

'I am sorry about last evening. But I promise that I will come with you today to listen to your Guru's words,' the second shopkeeper said.

That evening, as they walked down the cobbled street, he caught sight of that beautiful woman again. Once again, his pulse quickened and the blood rushed to his temples and his entire being was flushed with the excitement of the anticipated pleasure. Once again, he abandoned the idea of going to listen to the Guru.

'I am sorry my friend, I cannot come with you today too,' he said and he went up to his mistress.

This pattern was repeated each day and, every morning, the second shopkeeper could not but reflect upon how ephemeral his own happiness was when compared to that of his friend.

The first shopkeeper gave up talking to his friend about the sin he was committing and about the damnation of his soul. It was as the Guru had said: a state of grace would come to his colleague only when God willed it. Until that time, nothing on earth could bring him to the Guru. Each went his own way – the first following the path of grace and moving closer to spiritual salvation, the second following the path of sin and moving closer to eternal damnation.

Weeks passed. The fury of the monsoon had abated and Nanak's disciples, though they refused to admit it, knew in their hearts that their Guru would soon depart. This realization filled them with sadness and drew them even closer to him and led them to spend more and more time with him.

A few days before Nanak's departure, the second shopkeeper was supervising some renovation work in his house when a workman, digging before laying the foundation for a new wall, suddenly shouted that he had discovered that his pickaxe had dug up an object that had a dull shine to it as it caught the morning sun. The shopkeeper took it from the workman and rubbed it clean on the hem of his shirt. It was a gold coin.

There was excitement all around, but most of all in the shopkeeper's heart. He was sure now that he had stumbled upon a secret treasure of gold. The workmen were told to dig carefully around the place where the gold coin had been unearthed. After an hour or so, the workers did uncover a terracotta urn, the kind that is usually used for storing water during the summer months. The shopkeeper thought he would not be able to cope with the excitement. He was sure that the urn was full of gold coins; that the single gold coin that had been uncovered earlier had probably fallen out from the pot while it was being buried.

The workers dug out the urn and brought it to him. There was something bordering on reverence with which they handled it. The shopkeeper could not blame them, because he too felt something akin to awe towards the urn. It would make him richer than he had ever hoped to be. But he was hugely disappointed when he put his hand inside the urn and found only dust and ash. No matter how much he rummaged, there didn't seem to be any more gold coins to be found. He poured the dust and the ash out on the ground and one of the workmen sifted carefully through it. There was nothing in it.

There was disappointment all around. The workers had hoped that if an urn of gold coins had been discovered they would all have been beneficiaries of their employer's generosity in the form of a little bonus along with the day's wages. The shopkeeper, with his devil-may-care attitude was the first to recover from the disappointment. He flipped the gold coin in the air and caught it on its downward flight. He turned to his workers with a broad smile on his face and said: 'Well, I am richer than when I started out this morning!'

That day, the other shopkeeper was less fortunate. While returning from the evening satsang, he tripped on a stone, stumbled and fell. In the process, he narrowly escaped being impaled on one of a series of pointed stakes fixed in the ground to mark the boundary of a property on the side of the road. But though he had escaped what would have been a certain and painful death, he did not come away totally unscathed. A sliver of wood got embedded in his foot and could only be extracted by making a rather deep incision. The wound thus caused was covered with a paste of turmeric and mustard oil and bandaged. The pain persisted through the night in spite of the little ball of opium that the village *vaid* (a practitioner of Ayurvedic medicine) had given him and he limped to his shop the next morning. His friend was waiting to greet him with his usual effusiveness and to share the good news of his discovery of the gold coin. On noticing his friend's limp and

The Two Shopkeepers

the look of pain on his face, the smile left the shopkeeper's face, to be replaced with a look of deep concern.

'What happened my friend?' he asked.

The unfortunate shopkeeper told him about the sliver of wood that had got deeply embedded in his foot. His friend laughed in his face and said: 'You are the one who talks about reward and punishment for our deeds. You, who go daily to listen to your Guru and then work assiduously to practise what he preaches, should have been rewarded with gold not punished with such intense pain. I, who sin every evening in the arms of my mistress, as per your line of thought, should have been punished with eternal damnation. Instead I have been rewarded with the discovery of a gold coin. Your Guru could perhaps provide a justification for this.'

It was obvious that he was speaking in a tongue-in-cheek manner and drew great pleasure from what was a discomforting situation for his friend. However, the first shopkeeper showed no discomfiture at these words. He only smiled and said: 'If you can make the time to come and meet my Guru, I am sure he will be able to explain how this fits in with the pattern of God's working.'

That evening the second shopkeeper finally came into the Guru's presence. He listened to the *kirtan* and, when the congregation dispersed, the shopkeeper took his friend up to the Guru and introduced him: 'Master, this is my friend and neighbour. He is intrigued by what has happened to both of us recently and seeks your help in understanding the situation.'

The Guru listened to the question carefully, looking

all the time at the shopkeeper who was his disciple rather than at the speaker. When the speaker had finished, Nanak turned to him and said: 'Pain and pleasure are both given to us at God's will and with our limited understanding of His will, we are often left in confusion as to why we have been given one and not the other. You are right to think the way you do – the finding of the gold coin can be considered a reward and the piercing of the foot by the sliver of wood a punishment. But there is another way of looking at the situation. May be you were destined to find an urn full of gold coins but because you have given yourself so completely to the pleasures of the flesh and never sought to find comfort in singing the praise of God, the coins in the urn were turned to ash and dirt and you found only a single coin.'

Nanak added: 'Your friend was destined to be impaled on a sharp stake but because of the good deeds he has performed and his constant recitation of the Name, it was reduced to a sliver of wood in his foot. Man's life is determined by the actions he performs. If his actions are bad, he will only get a fraction of the good that destiny had in store for him. And if his actions are good, even the harm that was destined for him will be considerably mitigated. In any case, your friend has evolved far ahead of the desire of gold. He has through the virtue of his actions and his desire to keep God always in his heart found wealth of far greater value.'

After genuflecting to the Guru, the two friends walked away in silence, more than satisfied by the Guru's explanation. The second shopkeeper admitted in his heart that he had come face to face with a true Guru. He understood at last why his friend remained always in a state of bliss.

As hands and feet besmirched with slime,
Water washes white;
As garments dark with grime
Rinsed with soap are made light again;
So when sin soils the soul
Prayer alone shall make it whole.
Words do not the saint or sinner make
Action alone is written in the book of fate,
What we sow that alone we take;
O Nanak be saved or for ever transmigrate.

– *Japji, Pauri* 20[19]

Chapter 7

THE KUMBH MELA

INDIA IS A COUNTRY WITH PERHAPS THE GREATEST cultural and religious diversity in the world. Among the factors that bind the people of this populous nation together is the love that they share for festivals and fairs. Coupled with it is an obsessive fascination for pilgrimages. Throughout the year, especially during periods that are considered to be auspicious because of the special confluence of the planets, groups of people can be seen winding their way to the furthest and remotest corners of the country to pay their obeisance at the place of pilgrimage that is especially dear to their particular religious denomination.

A very special occasion arises when the pilgrimage and the fair come together and the event takes on epic proportions. One such event, as mentioned in Chapter 2, is the Kumbh Mela.

It is a mass Hindu pilgrimage of faith in which they gather to bathe in a sacred river. It is considered to be the largest peaceful gathering in the world and is held every third year at one of the four places by rotation – Haridwar, Allahabad (Prayag), Nasik and Ujjain. The Mahakumbh Mela is held at each of these four places every twelfth year. The Ardha (half) Kumbh Mela is held at only two places, i.e., Haridwar and Allahabad every sixth year.

The rivers at these four places are: the Ganga at Haridwar, the confluence (Sangam) of the Ganga and the Yamuna and the mythical Saraswati at Allahabad, the Godavari at Nasik and the Shipra at Ujjain. The name Kumbh Mela comes from Hindi, and in the original Sanskrit and other Indian languages, it is more often known as Kumbha Mela. *Kumbha* means a pitcher and *mela* means fair. The pilgrimage is held for about one and a half months at each of these four places where it is believed that drops of *amrit* fell from the *kumbha* carried by the Gods after the sea was churned. Bathing in these rivers is thought to cleanse one of all sins. There is no precise method of ascertaining the number of pilgrims bathing on the most auspicious day. Estimates may vary; approximately 80 million people, it is reported, attended the last Kumbh Mela at Allahabad on 14 February 2013.[20]

The origins of this *mela* are rooted in legend and mythology; it is impossible to say when it was first celebrated. Some say it was millennia ago and well before recorded history. Legend would have us believe that, hemmed in on one side by Durvasa Muni's[21] curse, which deprived them of their opulence and material wealth and on the other, by their ongoing war with the Asuras,[22] the demigods found themselves in a desperate situation. Lord Indra,[23] Lord Varuna[24] and the others held a conclave. Despite long-drawn-out discussions, they could find no panacea for their plight. So, they all assembled and made their way to the peak of the Sumeru mountain[25] where they threw themselves at Lord Brahma's feet and asked for his help. Lord Brahma, who is above all demigods and all-powerful, meditated till his mind was one with the Supreme Being.

On completion of his meditation, he advised the Devas to make their peace with the Asuras and obtain their help to churn the ocean. Among the valuable items that the churning would bring to them would be a *kumbh* containing *amrit* or the elixir of life, which would ensure immortality and would be their most potent weapon against the Asuras.

The Devas did as Lord Brahma had advised. In order to ensure that the Asuras cooperated with them wholeheartedly in this monumental task, they promised the demons a share of the elixir. The ocean was churned for a thousand years till it yielded the pitcher containing the elixir. The Asuras soon realized that the Devas had deceived them as they had no intention of sharing the elixir with them. A tussle ensued and, as mentioned earlier, while Garuda, the celestial bird, was carrying the pitcher away from the reach of the Asuras, drops of the nectar fell on the earth at four places: Haridwar, Nasik, Ujjain and Allahabad, each of which is regarded as holy and the pilgrim earns special merit in the eyes of God by making a pilgrimage to these places. That is how the obtaining of the elixir and subsequent triumph over the Asuras is celebrated by holding a *mela* by rotation every three years at one of these four holy places.

The final turn of the cycle, or the twelfth year, is celebrated at Allahabad or Prayag where the three holy rivers: the Ganga, Jamuna and the Sarawati have their confluence and the fair is called the Maha Kumbh. The Kumbh lasts for more than a month and, during this time, the various *akharas*, the religious sects and subsects set up their individual camps on the banks of the river, which together take on the ambience of a tented city.

Since it is mandatory for a pilgrim to bathe in the holy waters in order to make his or her pilgrimage successful, there are a series of auspicious dates and timings, the most auspicious of which is the Mauni Amasvaya,[26] when millions come down to the river to bathe.

The emphasis on bathing stems perhaps from the desire to cleanse oneself from the dirt of sins so as to be free from the vicious cycle of life and death and move towards a sphere where there is no suffering and pain. The congregation at the *mela* is motivated with the desire to achieve an eternal and sinless life and the bathing ritual is an attempt at ablution of our past sins. Other activities include religious discussions, devotional singing, mass feeding of holy men and women and of the poor and exchange of views in religious assemblies where various doctrines are debated and standardized.

On his *udasi* towards the east, Nanak found himself at Prayag at the time of the Kumbh Mela. He and Mardana set up a camp on a vacant piece of land between two *akharas*. In the evening, as prayers were being recited

The Kumbh Mela

and devotional songs sung at each of the many camps, Mardana too played his rabaab and Nanak sang hymns in praise of God.

The music was so sweet, Nanak's voice so pure and strong and the words of the hymn so beautiful, that some devotees from other camps too were drawn to the singing. Over the next few days, as the number of pilgrims increased, leaders of some of the other *akharas* too came. Nanak, with his usual politeness and open-mindedness, invited them to sing their bhajans as well. The devotees, who now thronged around Nanak, had the benefit of listening to songs in many voices and in many different veins.

Nanak, one of the wisest of men, would be in his element while taking part in the religious debates and discussions, which were an integral part of the *mela*. He loved this exchange of ideas and perceptions and, with the open mind that he had, absorbed and understood all the different opinions.

The other religious leaders, in turn, were impressed by the depth and sweep of Nanak's knowledge, understanding and wisdom and came to admire him. On the first day, when Nanak took part in one such discussion, a whisper ran through the group of raptly attentive devotees: 'Who is this strange man who is dressed neither like a Hindu nor like a Mussalman? We have never seen him before. Which *akhara* does he belong to?'

Soon the answer was found and a second murmur ran around the congregation: 'He is Nanak, the great Guru from Punjab. He travels far and wide to bring his teachings to the people.'

Initially, his teachings were considered strange because many of them did not subscribe to the traditional beliefs about religion held by the Hindus. Gradually, the simplicity of what he preached began to appeal to his listeners and to some of the leaders of the other *akharas*. People realized that what he preached was a way of life, which, if practised, would bring with it a strong measure of godliness. They also realized that what he preached were the simple precepts of all religions: to earn an honest living through the sweat of one's brow; to share what we have with others, especially those less fortunate then ourselves; to never consciously harm another; to perform *seva* (service); and to always keep God in our minds.

However, they realized that what was different in his teachings was the complete absence of any emphasis on rites and rituals. He seemed to be saying that spiritual merit was to be earned through our actions and the way we lived our lives and not through elaborate rituals. And yet, he never criticized the beliefs of those who did lay a great deal of emphasis on rituals. More and more devotees were drawn to the simple directions that he provided.

Though some of the leaders of the other *akharas* had come to admire him, many were jealous of the success he was achieving with his teachings while some others were bitter and angry because they saw some of their faithful devotees of many years standing being drawn to the stranger and his strange teachings. Hence, it was not surprising that they soon started a vilification campaign against him, accusing him of being an apostate who was deliberately misleading simple men and women and drawing them away from their religious beliefs. The loudest of these voices was from the leader of the *akhara* adjoining Nanak's camp who looked for every opportunity to belittle and criticize him. But by now Nanak's reputation as a man of God was too firmly entrenched in the minds of the people for the wild and bitter ranting of a jealous man to undermine it in any way.

Nanak would be awake well before dawn and spend an hour or two in silent meditation. On one such morning, his meditation was disturbed by a wild surge of people pushing each other to make their way to the water's edge. It was the day of the Mauni Amavasya, the most auspicious day of the Kumbh Mela and it was Brahma muhurta (early morning), the most auspicious time to bathe in the holy waters. It was imperative that all those who had come to attend the sacred festival should bathe in the river on this day and at this time if they hoped to attain salvation.

After a brief distraction caused by the initial surge of people towards the river, Nanak had turned again to his meditation. While he meditated, all those who had rushed down to the river returned after having completed the ritual, secure in the belief that the waters had washed away all their sins and they could resume their lives with a clean slate and the promise of an eternal life.

When they passed Nanak's camp, they were surprised and confused to find that he was in deep meditation and had not gone down to the river to bathe. The envious *mahant* (or head) from the neighbouring *akhara* too noticed it and saw in this an opportunity to destroy Nanak's standing amongst the pilgrims. He stood on a slightly elevated piece of ground and, pointing at Nanak, called out to passers-by and said: 'Come, come and see for yourself. There is now incontrovertible proof of what I have been saying all along. See the proof of this so-called Guru's apostasy. He is in Prayag on the banks of the holy Ganga on the most auspicious day of the Mauni Amavasya at Brahma muhurta, but he has not bothered to go down to the river and take the holy bath. What further proof do you need of his lack of faith and his lack of respect for our great religion?'

There was enough strength in the *mahant*'s argument to draw a small crowd of people to the spot. A few believed that Nanak would be able to offer an acceptable justification for his strange conduct. But a large number felt there could be no justification and were angry with the Guru. He had led them on to believe that he was a man of God but he had now provided proof to the contrary. The *mahant* continued with his harangue and soon the crowd around him swelled considerably. As the moments slipped by, an angry murmur began in the crowd, which gradually grew louder. At last, Nanak opened his eyes and smiled gently, first at the *mahant* and then at the crowd that had gathered around him.

In a soft, gentle but clear voice he asked the *mahant*, 'Why did you bathe in the river?'

'Why did I bathe in the river?' the *mahant* repeated Nanak's words incredulously. 'You know well enough why we all bathed in the river. It was to wash away our sins.'

'What did you wash with your bath?'

'My body,' the *mahant* replied not yet getting the drift of Nanak's subtle questioning.

'Did your body commit your sins?'

The *mahant* was quiet and Nanak turned and smiled again at the crowd. 'No, my friends. When we commit sins our body merely obeys the commands of our souls. If we wish to cleanse ourselves of our sins, then it is our souls, the real sinners, that we must wash and not our bodies. And can we cleanse our souls merely by taking a dip in the holy waters at an auspicious time? We can only cleanse our souls by making a permanent place for God in our hearts and in our minds. We hold evil thoughts towards other men in our minds and evil intent towards others in our hearts. If we are ready to cheat and steal and perform actions, which we know are wrong, how can the mere washing of our bodies make us pure? We will be like a brass utensil, which has been polished from outside till it blinds us with its brilliance, but, which inside, is filled with poison. Saints are pure and holy even when they do not bathe and thieves and murderers remain evil men even when they bathe four times a day. I am not questioning the faith of the people who believe that a holy bath at this auspicious time brings them in some strange way closer to God. All I am saying is that the holy bath should not remain a mere ritual but should be a precursor to a life well lived.'

As it had been in Haridwar, so it was at Allahabad. Nanak's preachings did not bring an end to the practice of bathing in the river, nor did it stop people from believing that a bath in the holy water at an auspicious time was the end-all and be-all of cleansing our souls of sins. But there was a small minority amongst that vast throng who were convinced by Nanak's words. The ritual of the holy bath could only be a beginning, the first step. Far more important in our quest for freedom from sin and the attainment of salvation was the way we lived our life after this first step. A good, well-lived life was what we must all aspire for if we want to achieve this goal. This small group of people would return home and spread Nanak's teaching among others.

He who is angry howls and is humiliated.
Blinded by wrath, he shouts in vain.
Says Nanak, it is best to remain quiet;
Without the Name all that the mouth
Utters is mere froth.

— *Raag Malhar, Chau Padas*[27]

Chapter 8

BAD VILLAGE, GOOD VILLAGE

𝒩ANAK AND MARDANA FURTHER TRAVELLED EASTWARDS, all the way to Assam. There are numerous stories in the Janamsakhis that tell us of the wondrous experiences that Nanak and Mardana had on their *udasis* and the many followers that they gained while travelling.

The journey back was as full of adventure as the outgoing one. It had been tough going, sometimes almost impossibly so. But over time, the long hours of walking had in themselves become a little easier and the duo had got accustomed to the blisters on the soles of their feet and the aching muscles at the end of the day. In fact, Nanak thought with a smile that once they got home they would miss this physical discomfort, which had become such an integral part of their lives. They had had to cope with the vagaries of the weather – the gruelling heat of the summer and the cruel cold of the winter, the non-stop rain of the monsoons and the unbearable humidity.

Things had been made worse by the fact that they had – out of necessity – to travel very light and all they had by way of belongings were satchels: each containing two changes of clothing, some emergency rations and their rosaries. There was nothing in them that would offer them protection from the changes of the weather, for which they had been dependent on the generosity of their host for the night, and this generosity had not always been forthcoming. Similarly, like all true mendicants, they had also been dependent for their food and nourishment on whatever people saw fit to give them. For the most part, people had fed them adequately, but, once in a while, they went hungry at the end of the day.

There had been homesickness too. Neither Mardana nor Nanak had ever been away from home for such an extended period of time and the memory of their loved ones would haunt them in the stillness of the night. Nanak, having achieved a state of grace, was able to accept this and live with it. However, Mardana could not. Often ,he would sob into his pillow and hope that his master would not notice his sadness. Of course, Nanak did notice. When the sobbing was too intense, Nanak would get out of bed, sit beside Mardana and gently caress his head. No words were exchanged but his master's hand upon his head brought a measure of solace to Mardana and the grief within him would be stilled and he would drift off to sleep.

Now, pondering over their journey and all the problems they had faced, Nanak had to admit that it was a small price to pay for what he had set out to achieve. In all the months that they had been on the road, there had not been and a single day when people had not come to listen to him; not a single day when people had not been influenced by what they heard. The journey with all its hardships had definitely been worth making.

The afternoon heat had softened as the sun went on the decline and it was time for them to move on. When they had been walking for a couple of hours and the cool evening breeze blew into their faces, Nanak knew it was time to plan their camp for the night. A couple walking briskly overtook them and Nanak asked how far the next human habitation was. Both the man and the woman looked churlishly at him and then walked on without uttering a word in reply.

'What strange people!' Mardana exclaimed.

Nanak smiled at the surprise in his friend's voice and said: 'You should not be surprised my friend. You know enough of human nature by now to know that it takes all sorts of people to make the world.'

A little while later, they stepped off the narrow road to make way for a bullock cart coming from the opposite direction. The bullock cart stopped a little way behind them and the driver got down and came running to them. He had obviously recognized Nanak as a holy man because he reached down and touched Nanak's feet.

'Where do you go, O holy one?' he asked.

'We have no destination. I travel to bring the word of God to whoever will listen and we stop to rest wherever the darkness descends on us. Could you be kind enough to tell us how far the next human habitation is? It is the place where we will have to spend the night,' responded Nanak.

The cart owner looked at Nanak with alarm writ large on his face and said: 'No master, you do not want to have anything to do with that place. The people there have forgotten God altogether and never take His name. The one temple that they have in the village has been allowed to fall into ruin and no one goes there to pray anymore. As a result, the people have forgotten all that is good and are not compassionate. They are full of their own egos and are all selfish, self-centred people. Because they do not know God, they have no idea of what kindness or politeness means. They are rude and unwelcoming to strangers. O no, you don't want anything to do with those people. It's far better to retrace your steps to the last habitation you crossed. It is still not too far away.'

The cart owner paused for a while and then, running his tongue over his lips to hide his nervousness, said: 'Perhaps you would consider getting onto the cart and coming to my home to partake of whatever little that I can offer.'

Nanak recognized the reason for his nervousness: it was the caste system at play again. He put his arm around the cart owner's shoulder and said, 'It is most kind of you my friend and you cannot imagine how deeply touched I am by your offer – it is both generous and unselfish – and God will bless you for it. Perhaps, if life permits our paths to cross again, we will be able to avail of your offer. But we must go on and take our chance and if the people of that village are what you say they are, then so be it. We've slept on empty stomachs before; it will not be something new for us.'

Nanak and Mardana resumed their journey and, late in the evening, came to the outskirts of what appeared to be a prosperous village.

Nanak stopped to rest under a spreading tree, and Mardana, unable to bear the intense pangs of hunger, went to scout for food and a place where they could rest for the night. He stopped at the first house he saw. The delicious aroma of food being cooked filled his nostrils as he peered into the house of an obviously well-to-do family. He knocked at the door and a handsome, middle-aged man emerged and came into the courtyard. As he came towards the door, Mardana realized that the man was handsome only in the arrangement of the features on his face and in the richness of his dress. Otherwise, the meanness in his eyes and the ugly scowl on his face made him one of the most unprepossessing men he had ever seen.

'Yes?' he asked and there was great harshness in his voice. 'What is it that you want?'

'I am a traveller and seek some food and a place to rest for the night for my master and for myself,' replied Mardana.

The scowl on the householder's face became deeper and he raised his hand as if to strike Mardana. 'Go away! What do you think this is: a *dharamshala*? I work myself to the bone to feed my family, not to give away food to wasters like you. Go before I strike you,' he yelled.

As Mardana turned away, the door was slammed shut and the bolt drawn with utmost urgency. Nothing could be more definite and final than this gesture.

Mardana made concessions for the man's behaviour; perhaps he was not as prosperous as he appeared to be, perhaps he had some vexatious problem on his mind, which had soured his behaviour. Mardana shrugged his shoulders. It didn't matter – it was a big village and surely there would be at least one generous soul who would offer them hospitality. Not everyone could be as rude and inhospitable as the man whose house he had just come away from, he thought. He was proved wrong. He received the same treatment – with minor variations – at all the houses he went to. As Mardana returned despondently to where he had left Nanak, he could not help recalling the words of the cart owner. The inhabitants had indeed turned their backs on God and on all the laudable traits of human nature that take us closer to Him. Rudeness and hostility seemed to be the special hallmark of this village. It was as if they had imbibed these negative qualities with their mothers' milk.

He wished now that his master had listened to the cart owner's advice and either turned back or gone with him. Nanak was deep in prayer and, not wishing to disturb him, Mardana sat beside his master and began to pray too. As he prayed, all the anger and bitterness at the conduct of the villagers and at the treatment he had received at their hands were cleansed from his heart to be replaced by a calm acceptance. It was as the Guru had said: 'It takes all kinds to make the world.'

Bad Village, Good Village

When Nanak finished praying, he realized that Mardana had returned empty-handed and knew that whats the cart owner had told them was true – the people had forgotten God: they should not have expected any kindness or hospitality here.

Night drew on and Nanak and Mardana wrapped themselves in their robes, curled up under the tree, and fell into an exhausted sleep.

They were up early and, after washing at a nearby well, sat down to pray before proceeding on their journey. When prayers were over, Mardana took up his rabaab, Nanak cleared his throat and started singing a *shabad* (hymn).

While they sang, a delegation of the villagers came to see them. All of them had sullen and sombre expressions on their faces and many of them were armed with sticks and axes. 'What do you want here?' the leader of the group asked Nanak belligerently.

Mardana opened his mouth to reply but Nanak held up his hand to indicate that he must hold his peace and let his master do the talking.

Nanak began speaking: 'Night fell while we were travelling this road and we stopped to rest. All we wanted was a little food to assuage our hunger and perhaps a place that would shelter us from the elements for the night.'

The leader grunted and brandished his stick in Nanak's face. In a voice loaded with hostility he said: 'Well the night is over and now you can safely resume your journey. Get to your feet and move on, there is no place for you here.'

'Was it too much to expect a little kindness from you?' Mardana said, unable to hold back a reaction to the treatment that was being meted out to them.

'Kindness!' the leader scoffed. 'Our kindness is towards ourselves, and this kindness lies in chasing away charlatans and parasites like the two of you as quickly as possible from our village. Who is to know what is in your minds – that you are not thieves, who would make off with whatever you could lay your hands on during the night? Or agents of a gang of robbers come to gauge the village? Be gone before we take the law into our hands and beat you to within an inch of your lives.'

Still, Nanak gave his radiant smile and said in the gentlest of voices: 'We have no desire to tarry here a moment longer. Come Mardana, we must be on our way.'

He got to his feet, retrieved his satchel with his meagre belongings and shuffled into his wooden sandals. Mardana did the same as the group of villagers watched them, still as sullen and as hostile as before. As Nanak turned to walk away from the village and the group of angry men, he held up his hand and said: 'May your village prosper! May you find so much happiness and prosperity in your village that you and your children never feel the need to go beyond its confines.'

The crowd was perplexed by Nanak's words. He had been treated with the utmost harshness and rudeness by the villagers and yet he offered them no word of rebuke but found it in his heart to bless them. They looked to their headman for a reaction but he was so overwhelmed and confused by Nanak's blessing that he was at a complete loss for words. Mardana was, of course, dismayed at his master's words. The scoundrels deserved no blessings, if anything they should have been the recipients of the vilest curses. But he had come to accept the strangeness of his Guru's words and actions on many occasions and so he held his peace. Nanak and his disciple walked away from the unfriendly village.

A few days later, as evening drew on, Nanak and Mardana found themselves approaching another small but fairly prosperous village. It was that magical time of the day, which in Hindi we call *gaudhuli bela* – for which there is no equivalent in English or, as I suspect, in any other language. It is the time of day when the cows and buffaloes return home from their grazing, raising dust with their plodding hooves. It is the time when the weary farmer returns home, his plough on his shoulder after a long and laborious day in the fields. It is the time when oil lamps are lit to dispel the gathering gloom and it is the time for the lighting of cooking fires. It represents a pause between the labours of the day and the stillness of the night. It is the time to take stock of the day's activities and to plan for a better morrow. It is the time for families that have been away from each other through the day to draw together and draw comfort and strength from each other as they eat their evening meal. It is also the time when the weary traveller looks for the gift of food and a place to rest his exhausted limbs to regain his strength for the journey of tomorrow.

On this particular evening, as Nanak and Mardana approached the village they crossed by a number of people, all involved in a cheerful exchange of the day's news, all willing to stop and greet the strangers. Recognizing Nanak to be a man of God, they all, without exception, bowed to him and touched his feet. As they reached the first habitation, they heard the ringing of temple bells and the sound of voices singing the evening prayer.

Nanak and Mardana had established a pattern for their travelling. They would eat their morning meal and set out on their journey. A short rest would be taken at mid-morning and, when the afternoon sun softened a little, they would resume their journey. As dusk settled in they would stop at the first human settlement they came to. Nanak would wait under a spreading tree and Mardana would go out in search of food and shelter. But on this particular evening, Mardana was spared this search. No sooner had Nanak settled under a tree, they were approached by an elderly gentleman. He had the lean, wiry frame that comes from working long hours in the fields. He greeted them warmly and, like all the other inhabitants of the village before him, bent down and touched Nanak's feet.

He said: 'I can see that you are travellers who have stopped at our village for the night. Honour me with your presence in my humble abode and partake of whatever poor food that I can offer you.'

His face was suffused with a radiant smile, as if the biggest achievement of his life lay in being able to offer Nanak and Mardana his hospitality. Nanak exchanged a swift smile with Mardana, who knew that, like him, his master too was thinking of the rudeness with which they had been treated a few days before.

Nanak and Mardana got up and they followed their host to his house. It was fairly large and comfortable, but not ostentatious. A cot was put out for them and warm water brought to wash their faces and their hands and feet. Nanak recited his Bani and the host's family members sat on the ground with their eyes closed and their hands folded in reverence even though the prayer (one of Nanak's compositions) must have sounded strange to them. By the time they had finished eating their evening meal, which had been simple but not lacking in nourishment, the chill of the evening had set in and the guests were ushered into a large, well-lit, simply appointed room. As they settled in for the night, tumblers of warm, sweet milk were brought for them and once again Nanak flashed Mardana a quick smile and Mardana knew that his master was making that comparison once again.

By the morning, word had spread of the holy man's presence and people of the village came in to catch a glimpse of him and to seek his blessings. Their host welcomed all the visitors and the conducting of a satsang flowed as naturally from this as a river flows down to the ocean. At the end of the satsang, there was such a strong feeling of well-being that their host begged them to stay on for a few days more and as all the villagers too joined their voices to this request. There was no way that Nanak could say no. For the next seven days, he stayed on and the villagers knew that they were singularly blessed by his presence and vied with each other to make him as comfortable as they could. Nanak found that the inhabitants were, by and large, honest and hard-working. They were God-fearing people who prayed regularly and they were kind and generous, sharing what they had with others.

As the week came to a close, the inhabitants of the village knew that he could tarry no longer and, on the eighth day, the entire village turned out to say goodbye to him. They followed him some way down the street and just before he reached the main road, Nanak turned to them and holding up his hand, blessed them: 'May your dreams and ambitions not be limited by the confines of your village. May your destiny take you far and wide and may you scatter in all directions in the realization of your prosperity and happiness.'

Mardana was startled by this strange blessing. He looked into his master's face for some clarity. But there was only the usual calm, serene smile. Mardana held his peace and the two went on their way.

In the days that followed, Mardana would find his mind going back again and again to that strange blessing and wondering about it, especially when he contrasted it with the blessing that Nanak had bestowed on that terrible village. There were times when Mardana found something inexplicable about his master's words and actions, but with the passage of time, he always found an explanation for this strange conduct and speech. However, but in this case, even after many days, he could find no explanation.

Then, one evening, he talked about his confusion to Nanak. 'Those who were rude, and mean and ill-tempered, you blessed with such prosperity that they would never have to leave home, never have to go beyond the limits of their village. Those who were the models of virtue, of kindness and generosity you virtually condemned to a state of exile. Why?' he asked.

To this, the Guru replied: 'They are such wonderful people that they will make a home anywhere and find happiness and contentment wherever they go. The explanation for my strange blessings is really very simple. Those who are rude, mean and vile in their conduct should remain confined within the limits of their village so that they do not colour the rest of the world with their rudeness and do not poison other people's lives with their vileness. Those who are kind and cheerful and generous and God-fearing should scatter far and wide so that their goodness illumines as many corners of the world as possible and the fragrance of their good deeds make fragrant even the meanest quarters.'

You bury your treasure underground,
But seek not Him whose treasury is boundless.
Those that spend their days in amassing wealth,
Go from the world without it.

– *Raag Gauri Bairagan*[28]

Chapter 9

THE STORY OF THE NEEDLE

NANAK AND MARDANA FINALLY RETURNED TO TALWANDI in 1506. Mata Tripta felt great joy on seeing her son again. During the long period of waiting for him, there had settled in her heart a deep sadness – the worry that she might never see her son again. Now, looking into his beloved face, the sadness lifted and in its place came a feeling of deep contentment: her son was back; nothing else mattered.

Nanak's reputation as a teacher and as a spiritual leader had spread all around and, even in his absence, his disciples had ensured that his word was spread further afield. So, when he returned to Talwandi, there were very few in the Punjab who did not know of him and his teachings. As word spread of his return, a large number of people made their way to Talwandi to seek his blessings and listen to his sermons. His lesson was simple and had instant appeal – hold faith in the one God and strive to do what is right.

Nanak ensured that he spent a fair amount of time with Rai Bhoe everyday. But there was a change in their relationship – though the Rai was older, he showed Nanak the deference that he would have shown to an older man. He could not help but look upon Nanak as his Guru.

Though Mehta Kalu's regard did not go so far, he had finally recognized that the greatness that Pandit Hardyal had predicted had at last come upon Nanak. And because of this, Mehta Kalu too was a little in awe of his son.

From Talwandi Nanak moved on to Sultanpur and here the same story was repeated. Nanki and Jai Ram were ecstatic to have their beloved Nanak back and large numbers of people thronged to Sultanpur to seek the Guru's blessings. His wife Sulakhani and their two sons, Sri Chand and Lakhmi Das, also joined Nanak here.

However, all too soon restlessness came upon Nanak again. He knew that his mission was far from complete and he needed to go forth again, this time in a different direction, to spread his message. So, after taking leave of his loved ones, he set out southwards, and as an early step in this journey, travelled to Lahore.

Lahore had by now taken on the position of a pre-eminent town of the Lodhi Empire, north of Delhi. Daulat Khan Lodhi, who had given Nanak employment when he first came to Sultanpur, had risen in rank to become the governor of Lahore and the adjoining areas. This was an important position and Daulat Khan had become one of the most powerful men in the empire, wielding a great deal of influence on the decisions taken by the emperor in Delhi. In spite of this, he never wavered in his respect and affection for Nanak.

The Story of the Needle

As luck would have it, at the time of Nanak's present sojourn in Lahore, Daulat Khan was away in Delhi for some important deliberations with the emperor. By now Nanak's reputation as a man of God was well established and, in spite of Daulat Khan's absence, not only did he have a large turnout at the evening satsang, but an important visitor too.

It was Duni Chand, the *amil* (revenue collector) of Lahore, one of the most important officials in the governor's court. He performed his duties honestly and, unlike other revenue collectors, fairly, without exploiting the poor. The governor had complete faith in him and they shared a mutual respect for each other, which resulted in a familiarity beyond what their stations in life would otherwise have permitted. Daulat Khan often talked to Duni Chand about his days in Sultanpur and, perhaps, inevitably, the talk would always turn to Nanak. So, Duni Chand was well aware of the respect and affection with which his employer regarded the holy man.

He came at dusk to Nanak's camp and, after touching his feet, said: 'O holy one, I have come with a special request and till you accept it I will not move from here.'

'Till you tell me what it is Duni Chand I cannot say if I am in a position to accept it or not. You may well ask of me something that is not in my power to give,' pointed out Nanak.

'It is my deepest desire that you honour my home with your presence. I wish that you stay with me during your sojourn in Lahore,' said Duni Chand.

Nanak was quiet.

'I am well aware of your proclivity of always residing with the poor and the underprivileged and I know how uncomfortable you are in the presence of wealth. But just this once I beg you to make an exception and come with me,' requested Duni Chand.

'You have the means to entertain thousands of holy men, mendicants and sages and ascetics. Why do you want me particularly Duni Chand?' asked Nanak.

'I would lose my job if your friend, the governor, were to learn that I had failed to play host to you while you were in Lahore,' Duni Chand replied.

Nanak smiled back. This pragmatic reason, he knew, was the clincher. Duni Chand was right. Daulat Khan would rant and rave if, on his return, he found that Nanak had not been given the welcome that he himself would have given him and Duni Chand would be the scapegoat on whom he would vent his anger. Nanak turned to look at his host and realized that if he did not go with Duni Chand and was hosted by somebody else, that host too would eventually have to pay the price. Nanak sighed. There was no way out of it; he would have to go with Duni Chand. He got to his feet.

'Forgive me, my friend,' he said turning to the poor man who wanted to host him too. 'It is not that I spurn your hospitality or that I find it in any way inadequate. But you heard what the *amil* said. If I do not go with him, he will be in trouble with his master, the governor, and I am sure you would not want that to happen.'

So shouldering their satchels once again, Nanak and Mardana followed Duni Chand to his *haveli*.

The Story of the Needle

Though the *haveli* was at the centre of the town, it was set in a large compound of its own. It reminded Nanak of the other *haveli*, Malik Bhago's in Saidpur. But the similarity ended with the size of the *haveli* and of the compound.

Duni Chand's haveli was marked by the constant hustle and bustle of the coming and going of people, by cheerfulness and gaiety. Nanak noticed that all the workers in the house had a cheerful, well-fed look about them, and their greetings to their master were accompanied with big, happy smiles.

Nanak and Mardana were made comfortable in a large, lavishly appointed room and their host fussed over them, taking personal care of their needs. He tested the water that was brought for them to wash with his own hands to ensure that it was of the right temperature. He sampled the food before they ate to ensure that the salt and spices were in the right quantities. All the time they were with him, his attention to their welfare never wavered.

Nanak observed him closely during his sojourn in Lahore and could not fault him on any but two scores. The first was the fact that, though he was essentially a good man at heart, Nanak noticed that he never attended satsangs nor did he ever see his host involved in prayers. He performed whatever rituals custom decreed, like the feeding of the poor and the holy ones on the prescribed days, but he did this in the most perfunctory manner, as if this was an onerous duty laid upon him and he needed to get it over with as soon as possible. Other than this, Nanak never saw him spending any time or effort in the true pursuit of God.

The second point on which Nanak could fault him was his obsession with amassing wealth and his inordinate pride in what he had succeeded in amassing. When he had brought them into his house and taken them to their room, he had taken pains to point out each piece of furniture and tell them how much it had cost. He told them how many people worked in his household and then, in the next breath, added how much it cost him to employ them. All around there were signs of great wealth and luxury and, if he thought that his guests had missed any of these, Duni Chand made sure to draw their attention to that particular item.

However, there was one strange item, which drew Nanak's attention again and again but about which Duni Chand offered no explanation. This was a set of seven red pennants (flags) strung across the front door of the *haveli*, which fluttered every time they were caught in a gust of wind. Nanak looked at them repeatedly as they fluttered: they were like captive souls seeking release, wanting to fly away with the wind, high into the open expanse of the blue sky, never to return. At last, when it was certain that their host would offer no explanation of his own volition Nanak turned to Duni Chand and asked: 'What do those red flags signify? You have not told us anything about them.'

'Oh those! They are a marker of my great wealth. Each flag stands for a lakh of rupees and I make every effort to add another flag every year or two. Soon I will have dozens of flags fluttering across my doors and windows and the whole world will stop and marvel at my great wealth,' Duni Chand explained.

The Story of the Needle

On their last night in the *haveli*, Nanak took Duni Chand aside and spoke to him privately: 'Duni Chand, you have been an exceptional host and have overwhelmed me with your hospitality and kindness. I have never known of any other officer of the court who put aside his work in order to look after two mendicants. Otherwise too, I have come to like you very much and to feel that you are a very trustworthy man. And because of my feelings for you I want to place in your care something that is of immense value to me; something that I cannot take on my travels for fear of losing it.'

Nanak took a needle from his satchel and handed it to Duni Chand and said: 'Will you take charge of this needle and look after it with the greatest care and return it to me when we meet next in the other world?'

Duni Chand was bemused by this strange request. How could a simple needle be so important for the Guru? But mysterious were the ways of holy men, sometimes beyond the comprehension of ordinary mortals like him. But no matter, if the needle was so important to the Guru he would guard it with his life till they met in the next world and he was able to return it.

The Guru left on his *udasi* and Duni Chand put the needle in a velvet-lined box as if it were a valuable piece of jewellery and locked it up with his other valuables in his vault. For the first few days, he basked in the pride that the Guru had found him worthy to be entrusted with what was obviously of great value to him. But this mood soon passed and he began to wonder what was so special about the needle. He would take the needle out of his vault at least three times a day and examine it carefully with the aid of a jeweller's eye glass. But try as he would, he could find nothing special in it – it was for all practical purposes, an ordinary sewing needle, the kind that any housewife had in her possession as a matter of course.

The more he pondered over the question, the more he failed to find an answer. Yet, he knew that there must be something very special about that ordinary looking needle. Why else would his Guru have asked him to take such good care of it not only in this life but also in their next life, till destiny ordained that they meet again? His failure to identify the special quality of the needle began to haunt him. He would tell himself again and again that it did not matter. It should be enough that the Guru had thought it worthy to be treated with such special care, it should be enough that he had been chosen as its custodian and its courier. But it was not enough. The question became an obsession and haunted him even in his dreams.

As the days slipped away, he found that his appetite too slipped away from him and he could not eat. His sleep became fitful and he would wake up and lie awake for hours on end, wondering about the nature of the needle that had been entrusted to his care.

He, who always had a cheerful smile on his face, now wore a perpetual frown. He, who had always greeted everyone cheerfully, now never even reciprocated any greetings from others. In fact, he looked angrily and churlishly at them and walked by without offering any reply. His work began to suffer and Daulat Khan, when he did finally return to Lahore and looked upon the change in his *amil*, was worried for him.

His wife, a sensible, level-headed woman had at first ascribed the changes in her husband to a professional matter, a financial loss perhaps. She had seen short periods of change like this before, and then when matters had righted themselves, she had seen him return to being his usual self again. She was sure that this too would pass. But when the days sped past and her husband's condition only got worse, she began to fear for him.

'What is on your mind?' she asked Duni Chand.

Duni Chand shook his head, made a brave attempt to smile and said in a barely audible voice: 'It is nothing. Don't worry about it. It will soon be alright.'

But it became worse and, every time she asked him about what was on his mind, she received the same answer, with minor variations.

One night, while Duni Chand lay awake, he heard his wife weeping, as if her heart would break. He was moved by the intensity of her grief. He reached out in the dark and drew her close and wiped the tears from her eyes.

He said gently: 'Hush. Don't weep. All will be well soon.'

'No, all will not be well. It's been over a month now but matters have only got worse. Tell me, my lord, what is on your mind?' asked his wife.

Duni Chand remained quiet.

His wife spoke again: 'We have been through so much together. We have seen both bad times and good and you have always treated me as your equal partner in your joys and your troubles. Why is it that now you hold back? I have never failed you in the past. I promise that I will not fail you now. Trust me.'

At last he opened up to her and said: 'You have always been by my side and, as you so rightly said, you have never failed me. The support and the love that you have given me have raised me to my present position in life. But the trouble, if it can be called a trouble, which has become the bane of my life, seems so trivial that I was afraid that I would be laughed at.'

She laughed softly.

'How often have we together laughed away troubles that were petty and trivial? Don't be afraid now, my lord. If your trouble is really trivial, why, we will together laugh it away as we have laughed away so much else in our lives,' his wife assured him.

So Duni Chand, at last, shared his concern with his wife. She was quiet for a while and then said: 'As soon as it is first light, show me the needle. Perhaps I will be able to see something in it which you have missed.'

Early next morning, they both went to the vault and Duni Chand showed her the needle. She looked at it carefully from every angle and then looked into his eyes. He saw the confusion there, a reflection of his own questioning. He offered her the eye glass but she shook her head. After a long silence, during which she continued to look at the needle, she turned to him and asked: 'Tell me exactly what the Guru said when he gave you the needle.'

He thought for while, taking care to ensure that he was able to recall the Guru's words correctly.

Mulling over each word that came to his mind he said: 'The Guru said that I must look after the needle very carefully, carry it into the next world and give it back to him there.'

She clapped her hands since she had finally solved the puzzle and said: 'You've been asking yourself the wrong question, my lord. The question is not what is so special about the needle. The question really is how you are going to carry it into the next world.'

Understanding dawned at last of what the Guru had tried to tell him by asking him to carry the needle into the next world and then return it to him. Of course, he could not carry the needle into the next world and, if he could not carry as infinitesimally small a thing as a needle, how was he going to carry the money, the gold, the silver and the expensive furniture that he had accumulated over the years?

He looked at his wife, smiled and, in a rare public exhibition of affection, put his arm around her shoulder and drew her close and did not let her go even though he was aware that a domestic staff member was already in the room.

The despondency fell immediately away from him and he was his usual self again. When life returned to the *haveli* at the start of the new day, the first thing everyone noticed was that the seven red pennants, that their master had been so inordinately proud of, no longer fluttered above the door. The captive souls had at last been freed. The next change that brought them great happiness was to see that their master was his old self again. He greeted everyone with his usual cheerfulness and once again wore a happy smile on his face.

In the days that followed, everyone noticed that only the veneer was the same, inside he was not really his usual self. He had changed and changed tremendously. He spent hours in prayer and in listening to religious discourses. There was no longer any pride regarding his wealth; there was no longer any desire to hang red pennants above his door. In fact, very soon people realized why the seven pennants had been taken down: the *amil* no longer looked upon those seven lakh rupees as his. He looked upon them as something he had held in trust for those who were in real need. Almost immediately, he began distributing the money among those who really needed it. And even when the money was exhausted, he continued to expend all his energies in bringing succour to the poor and the exploited. And through all these acts of piety and charity that he performed, his wife stood shoulder to shoulder with him, and the world marvelled at the perfect understanding that existed between husband and wife.

It is no surprise that both husband and wife became Nanak's devout disciples and when the Guru's *udasis* were over and the *dera* (camp or settlement) and the township at Kartarpur (details given later) were established, Duni Chand was one of the greatest contributors to these endeavours.

His goodness cannot be priced or traded,
Nor His worshippers valued, nor their store ...
Perfect His law and administration,
Precise His weights and measures;
Boundless His bounty and His omens,
Infinite mercy in His orders ...

– Japjee Sahib [29]

Chapter 10

THE FAQIR'S CURSE

From Lahore, Nanak made his way to Sialkot (about 125 km northwards), a bustling city that was situated in the foothills of the Himalayas. It is an ancient city and its founding is so lost in antiquity that the subject has become a rich source of myths and legends. The most popular of these legends would have us believe that the city was founded by Raja Sela, the uncle of the Pandavas.[30] This particular story goes on to tell us how it was rebuilt by Raja Satya Vachan, when it became part of the kingdom of Kashmir.

The earliest recorded mention of the city is found in ancient Greek texts going as far back as 322 B.C., where it is referred to as Sagala. We know that it was the easternmost point of the Hellenic Empire founded by Alexander and we also know that it became the capital of the breakaway Indo–Greek Empire. Sialkot was throughout this period famous for its silk.

Sialkot became a part of the Muslim Sultanate when Shahabuddin Muhammad Ghori captured Punjab in 1192. He was not able to conquer Lahore, but left a garrison in Sialkot, thus adding to its importance. At this time, many Sufi missionaries settled here thus making the Sialkot region a predominantly Muslim one and giving it a rich Sufi tradition.

From the earliest times, Sialkot had been an important post on the trade route between West Asia and Delhi and there was a constant hustle and bustle of merchant caravans arriving and leaving.

However, when Nanak came to Sialkot, there was no hustle and bustle in the streets. In fact, there was a strange quiet and, even when Mardana asked for directions, they were provided in whispers, accompanied by anxious over-the-shoulder looks, as if afraid that someone was watching, someone was listening. For a city known for its joyous activity and almost frenetic energy, there was a strange and unusual silence that seemed to have descended on everything and everyone.

Nanak set up base at the foot of an old *beri* (jujube) tree. Soon, with the stealth of thieves, people came to him in ones and twos, stealing quietly through the gathering dusk, walking almost on tiptoe and speaking only in hushed whispers and it was from them that he was at last able to draw out an explanation for the strange atmosphere that prevailed in the ancient city.

Here goes the story:

Though the city was inhabited predominantly by Muslims, there was a fairly large and powerful presence of Hindus, comprising mainly of rich businessmen and traders. Among these was a man by the name of Ganga who was well loved and respected by both the Muslim

The Faqir's Curse

and the Hindu communities. He was a pious, God-fearing man who gave away a fair amount of his income in charity. But in spite of his piety and his charity, God saw it fit not to bless him with a child. Many were the fasts that both husband and wife kept, many were the rituals they performed and many were the pilgrimages that they undertook, but all to no avail. Then, when they had almost come to terms with their condition and accepted the fact that they would never be blessed with a child, a visitor to their neighbour's house told them of the wondrous Sufi faqir, Hamza Ghaus.

'Nothing in this world matters to him: not pain, not suffering, not hunger and not cold. He spends all his time in prayers and in discussing the Sufi philosophy with other mystics and in his house he has built a small vaulted room into which he retreats from time to time to be alone with God. When he is in the room, no one is allowed to disturb him, not even to bring him food. Because of this mortification of the flesh and this solitary retreat, it is rumoured that he has direct access to God. He has more disciples than any other teacher of the Sufi philosophy and many people go to him with their problems and find help. It is said that he has come so close to God that God lends a special ear to his prayers,' said the neighbour's guest. He then went on to narrate how his own cousin had been blessed with a child due to the faqir's blessings:

> My cousin Hamida had no children even after twelve years of marriage. Finally, she decided to camp outside the faqir's home since she had heard so much about

him. Day after day she sat there, in the sun and the rain, unmindful of the cold of the night or of the hunger that gnawed within her. And all these days the faqir ignored her. It was as if he did not see her. But then, on a stormy night, when the wind roared through the trees, the thunder and the lightning seemed to be foreboding that the skies would split apart and the rain would drown the world, the faqir at last came out of his home to where Hamida sat. He drew her to her feet and led her inside and asked: 'Tell me Bibi what weighs so heavily on your mind? You have proved the earnestness of your purpose. What is it that you want from me?'

'I would have you pray for me – I want your prayers. I am a poor woman without parents or a brother or sister to support me and my husband has threatened to cast me aside because I am barren. Pray to your God Baba and ask him to bless me with a child,' said Hamida.

The faqir put his hand on Hamida's head and said in a soft voice: 'Go my child. My prayers now will be only for you, I will pray so long and so frequently that I hope God gives heed to my prayers and grants you what you so desire.'

Hamida came away and lo and behold! Two years later she was the mother of a strapping, healthy boy.

Ganga and his wife listened to this story with more than a little cynicism. They had tried it all: every potion, every concoction, every act of devotion and penance that holy men of every hue had asked them to perform. This would be just another item on a list already grown tiresomely long over the years.

The next day, Ganga's mother spoke to both husband and wife: 'I know you are tired and I understand how cheated and exploited you feel with all that quacks and pseudo-saints have practised on you and I don't blame you for feeling that the visit to the faqir will, like all that has gone before, draw a blank. But what harm is there in going? You cannot be in a worse state than you are already in. It is not men who work wonders but God working through men. Whom he chooses as his agent, always remains a mystery. Who is to say that the faqir is not God's agent till you go to him?'

So, with some reluctance, Ganga and his wife made their way to the faqir's unpretentious abode on the outskirts of the city. They took a cue from Hamida's story and camped outside the house. All through the day under the burning sun, and all through the night in the freezing cold, the couple sat patiently. They neither ate nor drank nor did they speak to anyone, not even to each other. They spent all those long days and nights in silent prayer.

Then, in the early hours of the morning ten days later, when both husband and wife had drifted into a brief, exhausted sleep, the faqir came out of his home and put his hands on their heads. Ganga and his wife woke up and the faqir, as he had done with Hamida, drew them gently into a sparsely appointed room in his house and asked them to lie down and get some sleep. As they lay in the holy man's abode, they found a strange peace and serenity descend upon them and everything that had seemed so important to them in their lives, now seemed trivial. They drifted off into a deep untroubled sleep. When they awoke a few short hours later, it was in a refreshed state of mind with no sign of exhaustion and fatigue of their ordeal of the last ten days.

When he saw that they were awake the faqir addressed them: 'What is it you want from me, a child?'

Even in the faint light of the early morning Ganga could see the mischievous twinkle in those large luminous eyes. It was as if the faqir was mocking the reputation he had begun to acquire in this particular direction.

'Don't believe in what people say. No mortal can promise you with any degree of certainty that you will have a child. Such matters are in the hands of Allah. If he wills, it you will have a child and, if he doesn't, then there is nothing any mortal can do to help you. Yes, I can intercede on your behalf. I can add my prayers to all the hundreds of prayers that you have already sent up to him and beg God to be kind and merciful to you,' the faqir said.

Though his words and mien were humble enough, a man more discerning than Ganga would have sensed a slight undertone of arrogance: an arrogance that came from knowing that he had met with frequent success in interceding with God on behalf of dozens of supplicants. Neither Ganga nor his wife sensed this; all they could see was that the holy man had agreed to pray for them.

The woman burst into tears, and Ganga close to tears himself said: 'That is all that we desire.'

The faqir insisted that they should break their fast

with him and they partook of the simple, spartan fare that he offered them. When they had finished eating and got to their feet to leave, the faqir turned to Ganga, with that same mischievousness in his eyes and asked: 'And what will you give me if my intercession with God is successful?'

'I will give you what I have most desired – I will give you my firstborn child. I will give him to you so that he can follow in your footsteps and become a man of God. Through his every breath, his every word and thought, his every action, I will be rendering thanks to God for his mercy,' replied Ganga.

There was nothing strange in this promise and Ganga's wife was not shocked or startled by it. Almost every childless couple, when praying for a child, promised the deity they were praying to, that they would dedicate their firstborn to his or her service. In case they were seeking a boon from a holy man they promised to give up their firstborn child to his ashram or *dera*.

The cynics would find a strange anomaly in this situation, because at the end of it all, the couple would again be left without a child. But this was not strictly true because even though they might not have the child living with them, the parents still found comfort and joy and some amount of pride in the fact that wherever he was, he was very much their child and that he was spending his life in the service of God. Historically, over 90 per cent of the parents who gave up their firstborn to God soon went on to have a second child and some even a third.

'Do not make this promise lightly my friend,' the faqir

warned. 'Remember that you are making a promise to God.'

Ganga shook his head and said: 'I do not make this promise lightly. I have thought on it long and hard and come to the conclusion that if God sees fit to bestow this kindness on me then this is the most apt way to express my gratitude.'

Like Hamida, Ganga's wife too bore a son two years later. Great joy filled the household. The mother's breasts ran full of milk and she found greater joy in suckling her baby than she had found in anything before. But when she looked down into that smiling contented face, she remembered what her husband had promised the faqir and she quaked with fear that he might fulfil that promise. The very thought made her heart churn. The child had been given to her after years and years of leading a childless life. But having received this gift and experienced what it meant to hold her child in her arms, she knew that she could never go back to living that childless life again. No, no matter what happened, she would not give up her child.

After the mandatory forty days of 'quarantine' of the mother and child, Ganga organized a celebratory feast and invited not only all his friends and relatives but also all the holy men of the city, among them faqir Hamza Ghaus too.

The faqir smiled when he came face to face with Ganga and the smile reminded Ganga of his broken promise.

'I have not forgotten my promise, holy one. But the boy is still too small. Let him grow up a little more and I will bring him to you and fulfil my promise to God,' Ganga said.

He knew that this was only a ploy to buy some time. Like his wife, he too couldn't find it in his heart to give up the child.

The faqir smiled again and said: 'The more you delay, the more difficult it will be for you to keep your promise. Remember this is no ordinary promise. This is a promise you made to God.'

The days flew quickly by. Ganga's wife found such joy and happiness with the child, such fulfilment that she was able to banish all memory of that fateful promise from her mind. But for Ganga it was not so easy. Most of the time, basking in the joy of his new-found fatherhood and in the intense pleasure that his wife found in the child, he was able to put the promise out of his mind. But sometimes, when he lay awake in the quiet of the night, it would come back to haunt him and he would be consumed by the anxiety of not knowing what punishment would be visited upon him. Finally, he confronted his wife.

He said, 'Remember our promise. If we do not fulfil it we will call upon ourselves the wrath of God. We are already remiss by delaying the act for so long. Let us go and give up the child to the faqir before God visits us with some terrible punishment.'

The mother clutched the baby closely to her chest and said: 'No. I will not give up my child. I will accept whatever punishment God chooses to visit upon me and I will accept it with a bowed head because I know that I have sinned. But I will not give up my child.'

There was such determination in her voice that Ganga knew there would be no shaking her resolve. And he was left to bear the anxiety and the uncertainty about the future on his own.

Then God himself intervened and gave him some relief. Ganga found that his wife was once again with child.

'Can we at least promise the faqir that we will give him our second child?'

'Yes,' his wife said without even thinking, too preoccupied with her son to think deeply upon the future.

Ganga made his way to the faqir's home. He was greeted with a cold, hostile look and his greeting was answered in the most perfunctory manner.

There was silence on both sides and then Ganga cleared his throat and made a tentative beginning: 'I know you are angry with me.'

'Angry is not the word,' the faqir said sharply. 'You made me your intermediary with God and you made a solemn promise to Him. Now you go back on your promise and expect me to greet you with warmth and affection!' he added.

He looked closely at Ganga, his eyes blazing with anger.

'I know I have sinned. I know that God will punish me. But think of my wife. The most important part of a woman's life is her love for her children. She was deprived of this for many years and now, at last, she has been granted this bliss. Try to understand how it is impossible for me to ask her to give up her child. I may as well be signing her death warrant,' explained Ganga.

'You said, when you made your promise that you had deliberated on it long and hard. Did you not then think of this aspect of the price you would have to pay?' the faqir asked.

'I did,' said Ganga in a soft, sad voice.

'Then you have betrayed God and because I was the one through whom the promise was made, you have made me betray God too. All we can do now is await the punishment that will surely be visited upon us for this betrayal,' the faqir said and turned to go back into his house.

'Wait,' Ganga said, putting a hand on his arm to restrain him. 'There is a way for us. Intercede for me again and ask God for another chance. He is all merciful. He will understand the feelings of a mother's heart. My wife is with child again. Ask God for his forgiveness. I promise that we will dedicate the second child to his service as soon as the forty days are over,' Ganga added.

'And you expect me to believe you after your betrayal the first time?' asked the faqir.

'I am not a man of God like you. I am a poor mortal with all the failings and weaknesses that mortals are heir to. I failed, I fell and I broke a solemn promise. I beg forgiveness and ask for a chance to redeem myself. It is really all that I, as a mere mortal, can do,' said Ganga.

He fell on his knees and burying his face in the hem of the faqir's robe, sobbed uncontrollably.

The faqir's heart thawed. Yes it was true, God was merciful and when a man admitted his mistake, begged forgiveness and asked for another chance, surely God, the all-merciful would forgive him and give him that chance. He raised Ganga to his feet, kissed him gently on the forehead and sent him on his way.

For the remaining months, till the second child was born, the faqir prayed to God on Ganga's behalf; he prayed long and often, till he knew in his heart that God had forgiven both Ganga and him.

Things, however, were not to turn out as the faqir had thought they would. Ganga had a second child and then a third and he made no move to give any of them up to the service of God.

With the passage of time, the fear of being punished by God seemed to have receded to some dim interior of Ganga's mind and did not seem to worry him at all.

Then, suddenly, one day, while walking through the market, Ganga came face to face with the faqir. They stopped for a moment, as if they would speak with each other. Ganga was too embarrassed to begin the conversation. The faqir, in turn, just fixed Ganga with a fierce angry stare and said nothing. The moment stretched on and then the faqir turned his gaze away and moved on and Ganga was left with a feeling of anxiety, which took the form of a tight knot at the pit of his stomach.

That night he had a strange and frightening dream. He saw himself alone on a desolate plain and at his feet were three dead bodies, wrapped in white shrouds. He stepped towards them and drew each of the shrouds away and looked into the dead faces of each of his sons. He woke with a start, the sweat streaming from his forehead, the ice-cold finger of fear placed firmly on his heart. The dream could well come true – this could be the punishment that God would visit upon him for his sin.

He found that he could neither eat nor sleep.

At last, when he could no longer bear the uncertainty and anxiety about the future, the constant worrying and the nightmares, he went to meet the faqir.

The faqir listened to him with an edge of impatience and anger. When Ganga had finished relating his troubles, the faqir pondered over what Ganga had told him and then he cleared his throat and spoke: 'God moves in mysterious ways and both his rewards and punishments take strange forms. This is your punishment for breaking your promise to him not once, but twice over. You will be haunted for the rest of your days by the fear of what might happen and this fear and what it does to you is your punishment.'

He was quiet for a while and then went on: 'The uncertainty of what might happen is always more frightening than what does eventually happen. I know this is a terrible thing to live with, a terrible thing to happen to anyone, but then you have committed a terrible sin and you must pay the price.'

He looked into Ganga's face and seeing what was coming next, he held up his hand and said firmly: 'Do not ask me to intercede for you again. I have interceded enough. I have made myself a party to your sin. Perhaps God has not punished me because he knows that I had no knowledge that you intended to betray him yet again. But he has seen fit to punish you and, if I intercede against this punishment, I am sure that God will not spare me any longer. Go now and live with this terrible punishment that you have called upon yourself. There is no cure for this ailment, neither with the men of medicine nor with the men of God.'

Due to this worry, which consumed him day and night, Ganga started losing weight, so much so that soon he was little more than a skeleton. He lost all interest in his business and confined himself to his house. He found it an effort to interact with his friends and relatives when they came to visit him. When people asked him what was troubling him, he merely shook his head and turned his face away. All the administrations of the most learned and famous of *vaids* and *hakims* failed to do him any good. Prayers were recited at his bedside. But though they brought him some measure of solace as he listened to them, the effect ended when the prayers came to an end.

Since holy men were being called upon to help Ganga, it was inevitable that an approach should be made to the faqir Hamza Ghaus too.

His friends and well-wishers went to call upon the faqir. But the moment he heard the purpose of their visit, he jumped to his feet and shouted: 'Go! Go away! Do not speak to me of that terrible sinner. He has sinned against God, not once but three times over.' And he told them the story of what had happened. 'I have prayed for God to forgive him on one of these occasions and God, the all-merciful, did forgive him. And yet he went and sinned again. I will not intercede on his behalf again, I will not ask God to forgive him yet again and risk inviting God's wrath on my head too. And you all also don't ever come to me on his behalf again. It is divine retribution that he has called upon his head and by seeking to intervene in

The Faqir's Curse

this, you will make yourself partners to his sins,' said the faqir.

Having heard the whole story, Ganga's friends knew that he deserved the punishment that had been visited upon him, most terrible as it was. They were also convinced that if anyone possessed the power to intercede for him with God, it was the faqir. Then the image of that awesome figure, drawing himself up to his full height and showing them the door, came back to their minds and they resisted for a while, the temptation to approach him again.

Ganga wasted away day by day and his friends saw him drifting closer to death before their very eyes. Soon the concern for their friend overcame their fear of the faqir's anger and, in the days that followed, groups of his well-wishers went with increasing frequency to the faqir to beg him for his intercession. Each delegation met the same fate as the first, but with the visit of each delegation, the faqir's anger became more terrible to behold. At last, when two delegations went to see him on the same day, his rage broke all bounds.

He stood in the centre of the market square and in a loud, powerful voice he called a curse upon the citizens of Sialkot: 'I have been plagued by visitors seeking my intercession with God on behalf of that terrible sinner Ganga. I had warned you again and again against doing this, but you have persisted in your folly. I curse you now. May the most terrible of plagues fall upon this town and may you all suffer greatly and for long. When the last of you have perished, may the city face total destruction till not a stone is left standing upon stone.'

A hush fell upon all those who heard him and they stood frozen where they were. Even when he turned and left the marketplace, they stood there in awed silence, overcome with fear at the enormity of the curse. The faqir strode to his house and went straight into his cellar to undergo the *chaliha*, the forty-day period of fasting and self-mortification that was necessary for the fulfilment of the curse.

Indian mythology and folklore are replete with stories of holy men and famous and highly venerated sages and sadhus, who when angered, have called down the most terrible of curses. As a result, deep in the subconscious of almost all Indians, there lurks the certainty that a holy man may not always have the power to help, but he certainly has the power to cause harm by cursing you.

The citizens of Sialkot had, over the years, invested the faqir Hamza Ghaus with supernatural powers, and they were now convinced that the faqir's curse would be fulfilled and nothing could save them from its fallout.

In the days that followed, an air of complete fear and dread fell upon the town and it was at this juncture that Nanak came to Sialkot. When he heard the story and garnered all the details from various people who came to see him, he sent Mardana to the faqir to ask if he could visit him. Mardana was met at the door by his chief disciple.

The Faqir's Curse

'I wish to meet the holy one,' Mardana said.

'The master is observing the *chaliha* and cannot be disturbed. There are still twelve days for it to end. Come back after these twelve days are over,' the disciple replied.

During the twelve days that he waited for the faqir, Nanak did what he could to allay the fears of the citizens by saying: 'Amongst the attributes that you credit Allah with, is the attribute of being all-merciful. You cannot possibly believe that a God who is kind and merciful would visit such a terrible curse upon you and your city.'

Nanak looked into the faces of the group of people who had gathered around him and saw that he had begun to make small tentative inroads into reducing their fear. He tried to quell their fears by saying: 'The faqir is a venerable man, highly respected and revered. He has always worked for your good. You know that well enough. But now he is angry, and quite justifiably so, for both Ganga and his friends have disobeyed him again and again, and in this anger, he has called a terrible curse down upon you. But knowing him to be a man of God, I am sure that during this *chaliha* he will be able to resolve this anger and when he comes forth, he will revoke the curse. Remember always that the faqir is a man of God and men of God will always seek the intervention of Allah, the all-merciful, to do you good, not any harm.'

He fell silent again to let the import of his words sink in. Each person pondered over what Nanak had just said. It was true that the faqir had always worked for their good. If he was angry with them now, his anger was justified. But those who had seen that awesome display of anger in the marketplace still feared the worst and were not altogether reassured by Nanak's words.

In the evenings, over the next twelve days, Nanak gently and subtly drew the gathering away from their fear and made every effort to diffuse the impact of the faqir's terrible words. He won many converts and admirers with his soft, gentle words and his humble ways. More and more people were drawn to his simple teachings, expressed in simple words, which everyone could understand. The path to salvation that he showed them was one that they recognized – the path that all good people tried to follow in their pursuit of goodness. There was no room for any anger or harshness or fear in what he taught. The words he preached were warm and friendly and comforting, with a total absence of talk of catastrophic punishments or avenging angels. By the time the faqir emerged from his self-imposed mortification, Nanak had garnered a large number of followers, cutting across faiths.

The faqir sat down to break his forty-day-long fast. Barely had he put the first morsel of bread into his mouth, when one of his disciples informed him of Nanak's presence in Sialkot. The faqir immediately abandoned his meal, washed his hands and set out to meet the Guru. He had heard much about Nanak and his teachings over the years.

Nanak saw him coming towards the *beri* tree and, from his clothes and from the emaciated look on his face, he knew him to be the faqir. He, in turn, had heard a great deal about the faqir, about his piety and about his constant striving for the good of the people. He observed no distinction of caste and creed and was uniformly liked and respected by people of all faiths. Nanak had such a deep regard for the faqir that even the current sad episode of him cursing the town of Sialkot could not dilute it. He understood the anger that had occasioned the calling down of the curse. Like so many other sadhus and faqirs that Nanak had come across, the spiritual powers that he had come to possess had, on occasion, made the faqir forget his humility. In the current situation, it was anger at being disobeyed – how dare Ganga and the other citizens of Sialkot, who were ordinary human beings, disobey a spiritually powerful faqir like him? This would pass, once the mood of arrogance had been pushed aside.

Seeing him approach, Nanak got to his feet to greet him and when they were near enough he drew him into a warm embrace.

They sat side by side in the shade of the tree and exchanged a few pleasantries. The faqir apologized for not being there to welcome Nanak on his arrival and said: 'I was observing the *chaliha* and could not be disturbed.'

'Yes, I heard about the *chaliha* and about the terrible curse you have laid upon Sialkot and its inhabitants,' observed Nanak.

'You do not approve? I can hear your disapproval in your voice and see it in your eyes,' said the faqir.

'With your prayers, your meditation and your periods of self-mortification you have become a highly evolved spirit – it would not be possible for any man to hide from you what was lurking in his heart. Yes, I do disapprove,' clarified Nanak.

He paused, but the faqir was silent, waiting for the Guru to go on.

'For me there is no room, in my concept of God, for the kind of retribution that you are trying to call upon the citizens of Sialkot. For me God is good and kind and the epitome of mercy. For me He exudes love and peace. My God would listen to the prayers of the holy ones when these prayers were offered seeking help and mercy for ordinary mortals. He would never listen to a prayer that asks Him to visit such a terrible punishment on an entire town full of people. If you do seek punishment, it should be for the sinner Ganga, though God knows, the poor man has been punished enough. He alone is guilty. He made a solemn promise to God with you as witness and he broke that promise not once but twice. He has sinned, but, in seeking to punish him, you should not punish all the others. In every group of people you find both: the sinners and the virtuous, the foolish and the wise. Amongst the citizens of Sialkot too, there must be many who are wise and virtuous and God-fearing. It is not fair that your curse should embrace them too,' Nanak finished saying.

'No,' the faqir said firmly. 'They are all foolish sinners, every last one of the citizens of Sialkot. And they all deserve the dire punishment. They sinned by ranging themselves on Ganga's side against the verdict of God.'

Nanak did not argue any further. He asked Mardana to give him two slips of paper. On one he wrote: 'Falsehood' and on the other he wrote: 'Truth.'

'Mardana go to the market and buy one paisa worth of

The Faqir's Curse

each of these commodities.' A paisa was no mean amount of money in those days.

Mardana was quite mystified by his master's 'shopping list'. But he knew he had to carry out Nanak's bidding. Perhaps there was something in the slips he did not understand, perhaps the shopkeepers would know what Nanak wanted – they usually knew even about the most rare and exotic commodities that the odd customer might demand. He looked around the marketplace and saw that the second shop to his right was kept by a young, sweet-looking shopkeeper who smiled encouragingly when he found Mardana looking in his direction.

'Can I do something for you?' he called out helpfully.

Mardana felt fairly certain that the shopkeeper would be able to help him. He went into the shop and handed the two slips to the young shopkeeper. The shopkeeper peered closely at the two slips in turn, a deep frown forming on his brow as he read the slips, not once but over and over again. Then he looked up at Mardana and asked: 'What kind of joke is this?'

Mardana searched for words to explain that his friend and master never joked regarding such serious matters. But before he could find the appropriate words, the shopkeeper raised his hand and shouted: 'Get lost before I hit you.'

Mardana beat a hasty retreat. He stopped on the other side of the square to take stock of his situation. He looked at the slips again. They still made no sense to him: How on earth could you buy one paisa worth of truth and one paisa worth of falsehood? He didn't blame the shopkeeper for his reaction. Perhaps an older and wiser shopkeeper might be able to help. He looked around and found a venerable looking shopkeeper peering over his counter in his direction. He had a skull cap on his head and a flowing henna-stained beard, and on his face there was the mark of years and years of having traded in a vast variety of commodities. If anyone knew what the 'truth' and 'falsehood' in the slips stood for, it would be this man.

Mardana put his experience with the first shopkeeper out of his mind and, going up to the old man, greeted him politely, 'I am confused. My master has given me these two slips but no one seems to understand what they mean.'

The shopkeeper took the slips from Mardana's hand and peered closely at them. And while he tried to decipher their meaning, he lifted up his skull cap and scratched his head as an expression of his perplexity. Then he shook his head and handed the slips back to Mardana and said: 'I am sorry my friend. I can make nothing of these.'

At all the other shops he went to, Mardana met with varying shades of the reactions that he had witnessed at the first two shops. At last, when he began to despair of ever taking back a paisa worth of falsehood and a paisa worth of truth to his Guru, he came to a shop owned by a shopkeeper named Moola. Moola was a God-fearing man, well known for his wisdom and sagacity. Young businessmen, just starting out on business, would often turn to him for advice. Even ordinary citizens of Sialkot sought him out when they needed help in investing their wealth or utilizing their resources.

Embarrassed by the reception he had received at all the other shops, it was with a great deal of diffidence that

Mardana approached Moola, who took one look at the slips and smiled.

Moola said: 'Wait. I'll just get them for you.' He went into the room at the rear of the shop and, after a minute or two, came back with the slips and returned them to Mardana.

'Here you are.'

Mardana looked at the slips and then at Moola. The shopkeeper, on sensing Mardana's confusion clarified: 'They are on the reverse of the slips.'

Mardana turned them over. On the reverse of the slip that had falsehood written on it, were the words: 'Life is false.' And on the reverse of the other was written: 'Death is the truth.'

'Now give me the two paisas,' he said with a smile and Mardana handed the coins to him.

He returned to Nanak's camp and handed the Guru the two slips of paper. Nanak read what was on them and passed them on to the faqir. The faqir looked long and hard at what had been written upon them. Then he looked up at Nanak and there was a gentle smile playing at the corners of his lips.

'You make your point well, O holy one. As long as there are people who can think and feel like this, virtue, wisdom and goodness will flourish in Sialklot. I cannot seek to punish an entire city for the perceived sins of one citizen,' conceded the faqir.

He paused for a moment and then went on, 'But even more than that, you have made me see that in my overbearing arrogance, I had forgotten the compassion towards all mankind, especially towards those who have fallen, which followers of all Sufi traditions practise. I had forgotten that inner humility in one's heart is next to godliness. I had forgotten that God is always kind and merciful and compassionate and would never subscribe to the anger and hatred that motivates my curse. In fact, I have demeaned myself in the eyes of God by trying to lay this curse on the people of Sialkot.'

Soon, as publicly as he had made it, the faqir retracted his curse.

Nanak also convinced the faqir that Ganga too had suffered enough and thus paid the price for his sins. Together they went to the sick man's bedside and, through their ministrations and their prayers, restored him to good health.

What became of Moola the shopkeeper? He had followed Mardana and had come face to face with Nanak. In the days that followed, he spent all his time with the Guru and became an ardent devotee.

When the time came for Nanak to move on, almost the entire citizenry of Sialkot was there to see him on his way. There were many in that crowd who now firmly believed that the path that Nanak preached to salvation was the right path.

If you have the musk of virtues,
The fragrance will be secreted.
If such virtues are obtained from a friend,
These may also be shared . . . .
Wherever you go, do sing His praises.
Skimming nectar with every phrase,
If you have the musk of virtues,
The fragrance will be secreted.

– *Suhi I, Chhant,* Section 4[31]

Chapter 11

THE BOWL OF MILK AND THE JASMINE PETAL

ON HIS JOURNEY SOUTHWARDS, NANAK CROSSED THE river Sutlej at Bhatinda and spent four months with Sufi saints of the town. The Janamsakhis tell us that he preached what he had taught faqir Hamza Ghaus: that compassion and piety were more becoming to men of God than the exercising of occult powers.

Then he visited the Jain temple of the Dhundia sect at Bikaner and interacted with the head priest. Nanak countered the widely held Jain belief that someone who ate new and whole grains, drank unstrained water and broke and ate the fruit from the trees destroyed life and would be condemned to eternal damnation. He said that life and death, suffering and joy were all in the hands of God and that to believe in superstitions was a sin.

His next important stop was Ajmer, where he discussed metaphysical issues with the Sufi leaders at the dargah of the saint Khwaja Moiuddin Chishti. He preached to a large gathering at the *mela* (fair) in nearby Pushkar on Baisakhi day[32] (14 April).

He then moved on southwards passing through Mount Abu, Ujjain, Indore and other important cities till he came to Rameshwaram (now in Tamil Nadu). From here he sailed to the port of Trincomalee in Ceylon (now Sri Lanka).

Ceylon was, at that time, according to its history, divided into three kingdoms: Jaffna, Kotte and Kandy. Both Kotte and Kandy were Buddhist kingdoms and their population consisted almost entirely of the original, ethnic Sinhalese population. Jaffna in the north was close to the Malabar coast and, had over the centuries, received a large number of Indian immigrants. These were mainly Hindu Tamils. By the time Nanak reached Sri Lanka, Jaffna had a predominantly Hindu Tamil population along with a fair smattering of immigrants from other parts of India, mostly traders and craftsmen from the Indo-Gangetic region.

Among them was an extremely skilled jeweller called Mansukh. He attracted the attention of the king, Shivnabh (also known as Shivnath), and his queen not only by his great skill and craftsmanship but also by his personality and the manner of life that he led. They were impressed by the radiance that shone on Mansukh's face and by the gentleness that was reflected both in the way he spoke and in the way he conducted himself.

Though born Hindu, he did not practise any of the prescribed Hindu rituals. He did not visit temples or indulge in the worship of idols. He did not observe any of the fasts nor did he practise any of the austerities.

He told them that his Guru called Nanak had taught him that, since there is one God and he is formless, there is no merit to be earned in the performance of meaningless rituals and penance; merit can only be earned by living a virtuous and righteous life.

The more the royal couple learned about Nanak, the keener they became to meet him.

It was at this juncture that Nanak arrived in the city and soon word spread that a holy man from North India had come. Shivnabh too heard the news and his heart beat with excitement. Perhaps it was Guru Nanak; perhaps this was the arrival that he and his wife had been waiting for.

The next morning, Shivnabh accompanied by the queen, went to visit the Guru. After they had listened to him for a few minutes, the royal couple was convinced that they were indeed in the presence of the one they had been eagerly waiting for. They threw themselves at Nanak's feet and became his disciples.

In the days that followed, the royal couple spent endless hours with Nanak in the discussion of metaphysical issues and Shivnabh found answers to questions that had plagued him for years.

It was not long before Nanak noticed an underlying sadness that lay beneath everything the queen said or did. He realized that it was because she had no child. At an opportune moment he offered her solace by saying: 'This is God's will and you have to accept it with the same grace and dignity with which you accept his blessings. God gives us ten things but holds back one. That one thing assumes such importance that we forget to be grateful for the ten things we have been given. We forget that he could easily take away the ten he has given us and there is nothing that we can do about it. Think of your subjects as your children and give them the same love and care that you would lavish on your child. You will thus find fulfilment for your thwarted maternity. Perhaps this is the reason why God has not seen fit to bless you with a child: so that you can love all your subjects as your children.'

The queen did as Nanak had bid and, in showering her unstinting love on her subjects, she found the fulfilment that had been denied her. Nanak saw with the passing days the sadness lift from her being only to be replaced by a stillness of spirit and an all-pervading joy.

In gratitude for the peace and contentment that Nanak had brought to their lives, Shivnabh built a magnificent *dharamshala* so that the Guru's disciples could conduct their satsang even during inclement weather.

Soon it was time for Nanak to move on. It was a tearful congregation that bade him goodbye and the queen wept as if her heart would break. Nanak offered whatever reassurance he could to everyone and then went on his way.

Before returning to India, Nanak visited other parts of Ceylon, amongst them: Katargama, Sitawaka, Mannar and Anuradhapura.

On his return journey he crossed the Palk Strait and travelled along the Western Ghats passing through Kumta, Ankola, Dharwar, Nasik, Ankleshwar and on to Junagadh, Porbadnar, Dwarka and Bhuj. He crossed through Rajputana and the south-west Punjab till he came to Multan, which is now in Pakistan.

The Bowl of Milk and the Jasmine Petal

Multan is one of the oldest cities in South-East Asia. The greatest advantage it has is its geographical location. Three rivers merge here before passing on their way to join the Indus. Hence, it was relatively cheap and easy to travel down the river all the way to the Arabian Sea, both for passengers and cargo. Multan was easily accessible by land as well. As a result, it soon became a commercial hub for national and international trade, including with Persia, Central Asia and the Arab world.

During the time of the Mahabharata, it was the capital of the Triganta kingdom and was ruled by the Katoch clan of the Kshatriya Rajputs.

Legend has it that when Alexander attacked the city with a view to capturing it, he was hit by an arrow and was so severely injured that he fell unconscious. Enraged by this, his armies renewed their attack with greater vigour and Multan soon fell to the Greek invaders. Alexander never recovered from the wound, which was to prove fatal. For the next thousand years, Multan was ruled by Hindu and Buddhist kings and was a part of both the Maurya and the Gupta empires. Heun Tsang, the famous Chinese traveller visited Multan in A.D. 641.

During this early period, Multan was also known as the 'city of gold' because of the wealth in its many temples, the most famous being the Suraj temple. Claimed to be by far the biggest temple in the subcontinent, many historians have described this legendary temple and its fabulous wealth.

During the second half of the seventh century, Multan had its first experience with the marauding Muslim armies.

The temples were raided and looted of their gold and the inhabitants were taken captive to be sold into slavery.

Muhammad bin Qasim, one of the earliest Muslim conquerors, not only captured the city and raided the temples, but also brought it for the first time under Muslim rule. During the eleventh century it fell prey to Mahmud Ghazni's[33] rapacious plundering and to his obsession with the destruction of Hindu temples. He not only damaged the Suraj temple and destroyed the giant idol but also carried away an immeasurable quantity of gold. The Arab geographer and scholar, Al-Baruni, who wrote an account of India and spent much time at Mahmud's court, has described the desecration, destruction and plunder of the temple in graphic and gory detail. He wrote of his raids that 'the Hindus became like the atoms of dust scattered in all directions . . . . They have the most inveterate aversion towards all Moslems.'[34]

When another invader, Muhammad Ghori, set up his kingdom with its capital in Delhi, Multan became a part of it.

Perhaps, in reaction to the fact that Multan had once been a stronghold of the Hindu religion with myriads of temples dotting the landscape, each Muslim conquest resulted in the building of more mosques and the setting up of more seminaries. This went on till the town was studded with mosques the way it had once been studded with Hindu temples. Mosques and seminaries also dotted the countryside around Multan.

During the twelfth century, many Sufi scholars made Multan their base and the process of conversion of the population of the area to Islam gained momentum in the early thirteenth century. There is reason to believe that these conversions were by and large voluntary, spurred on by the renunciation that the Sufi saints practised and by the basic Sufi tenet, which preached the equality of all human beings. The Sufi sects (called *silsilas*) not only gave a sense of belonging and togetherness to those who subscribed to that particular order but also drew the praise and admiration of those outside the order. The *khanqah* or meeting place and residence of the Sufis gave a chance to both Muslims and Hindus to listen to the Sufi teachings, which dwelt so firmly on the brotherhood of man, thus attempting to bring the two communities together.

By the time Nanak came to Multan, the city was famous as a major centre of Sufi learning and philosophy. Each Sufi sect had established a strong base in the city and each of the schools of Sufi thought vied with each other to gain pre-eminence.

Though the Sufi practice is the gentlest and most tolerant of the many streams of Islamic thought and practice, there had set in, among the Sufi schools in Multan, a sense of rivalry, in their quest to draw more and more followers to their particular school of thought.

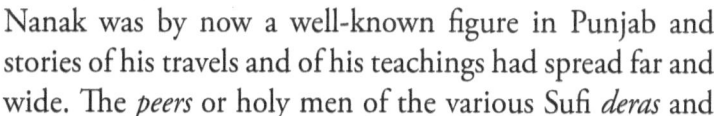

Nanak was by now a well-known figure in Punjab and stories of his travels and of his teachings had spread far and wide. The *peers* or holy men of the various Sufi *deras* and dargahs in Multan had followed his growing popularity with detached and objective interest. As long as he did not come to Multan to gain converts, his growing popularity and following was no cause of concern for the Sufi *peers*.

Nanak was still at two days' walking distance from the city and had set up camp in the house of a cobbler in a small village. As always the people had at first regarded him with suspicion, afraid that he would try to wean them away from their religion. But, when they listened to his Bani, they realized that for the most part he was merely reinforcing what their own religion taught them and warmed up to him and to what he was trying to say. As was so often the case, they begged him to stay on a few more days.

Amongst the gathering, during the early days of Nanak's sojourn, was a citizen of Multan, who had come to visit a relative. When he rode back to Multan, he took with him stories of how the people had been so impressed by Nanak's teachings that more and more turned out to listen to him. He also took back the information that Nanak would next be setting up camp in Multan.

This news caused alarm among the Sufi faqirs. As long as he was preaching elsewhere in the Punjab, they had not looked upon him with anything other than a patronizing tolerance. But now that he was coming to Multan to preach, he would impinge on their spheres of influence and pose a decided threat to their own position and standing. They already had a difficult time holding their own against each other; it would never do to have an outsider come in and make things more difficult for them.

The Bowl of Milk and the Jasmine Petal

The oldest and seniormost of the Sufi clerics called for a conclave of all the heads of the *silsilas*. For once, they decided to bury their personal differences and put up a common front against this impending threat. The conclave stretched over the next four days. Stories of how rapidly Guru Nanak had gained followers were repeated and various ways and means were suggested to keep him away from Multan.

At the end of these deliberations, a consensus had emerged that it would never do to express any hostility or open resistance to Guru Nanak or his teachings. Time and again, they had heard stories of how such hostility and resistance had always been counterproductive and resulted in a greater spurt of growth in his popularity. In any case, their own schools of thought preached against all forms of hostility and an expression of anger was essentially abhorrent to most of them. It was left to the seniormost dervish to devise a way to let Guru Nanak know that he was not welcome in Multan: a way that was at once both subtle and sensitive.

The dervish was nothing if not a master at subtlety. So, late one evening, when Guru Nanak finally approached the gates of Multan, he was greeted by a delegation of young Sufi acolytes with warm smiles and a collective gift from the heads of various Sufi *silsilas* of Multan. The gift, which was carried with extreme care, was an earthen bowl, filled to the very brim with milk. One careless or hasty step by the one who carried it, and some of the milk would have spilt.

Nanak looked at the gift and then at Mardana.

'Why master,' Mardana asked in a whisper. 'The milk is not sufficient to provide sustenance to even one of us. Why did they not bring something more substantial?'

Nanak smiled at Mardana. He knew enough of the Sufis and their way of thinking to know that they always gave their message through subtle allegories. He understood what was sought to be conveyed to him and reached out to the jasmine bush growing besides him. Plucking a single petal, he placed it gently on the surface of the milk.

'Please take this back to your masters as a gift from me,' Nanak said to the acolytes.

A couple of the acolytes smiled, first at Nanak and then at each other, and he knew that they had understood the import of his gesture. They turned and walked back to the city, carrying the bowl of milk as carefully as when they had carried it out of the city.

'What was that about master?' Mardana asked even more confused by what his Guru had just done.

'They sent me a bowl filled to the very brim with milk. If one tried to add even a drop more, the milk would overflow. They were telling me that Multan already had as many religious teachers as it can contain. Adding even one more would result in a displacement,' Nanak explained.

'And the petal of the jasmine flower?' asked Mardana.

'That was to tell them that I have no intention of displacing anyone. I will come as gently amongst them as the petal of the jasmine flower had come into the bowl of milk. If anything, my effort would be only to add, if I could, a fragrance to their teaching, just as the jasmine petal had brought a fragrance to the milk,' explained Nanak.

Nanak came to Multan and the Sufi teachers found that he was true to his word. He did not preach against any of them and did not create any rivalries. He himself often came to them to learn. He did not cause any kind of displacement and instead brought a fragrance that permeated the entire atmosphere of religious learning and debate in the city. So perfect was the harmony that he established with all the leaders of the various *silsilas* that when he did finally leave Multan, they were sorry to see him go.

The bowl of milk with the petal of the jasmine flower was not only a message of reassurance to the Sufi leaders of Multan but also a symbol of the way we should lead our lives in relation to those around us.

Nanak then went to Pak Pattan, a town near Sirhind. It was the seat of Hazrat Khwaja Farīduddīn Mas'ūd Ganjshakar (1173–1266), popularly known as Baba Farid or Sheikh Farid, the famous Sufi saint and Muslim missionary, belonging to the Chishti order. He spent many days there holding discussions with him. Later, he personally included 134 hymns composed by Baba Farid in the Adi Granth, the most sacred scripture of Sikhism.

Here it must also be mentioned that 'one of Farid's most important contributions to Punjabi literature was his development of the language for literary purposes. Whereas Sanskrit, Arabic, Turkish and Persian had historically been considered the languages of the learned and the elite, and used in monastic centres, Punjabi was generally considered a less refined folk language. Although earlier poets had written in a primitive Punjabi, there was little in Punjabi literature apart from traditional and anonymous ballads. By using Punjabi as the language of poetry, Farid laid the basis for a vernacular Punjabi literature that would be developed later, as a regular language.'[35]

Tilla Baba Farid (the city of Faridkot in Punjab) then known as Mokhalpur was named after him by its then ruler Raja Mokhal. The festival Bābā Sheikh Farid Āgman Purb Melā is celebrated each year for three days, from 21 to 23 September, commemorating his arrival in the city.

From Pak Pattan Nanak travelled back to Talwandi. His parents, now grown old, were happy beyond words to see their son after so long. Because of him, Talwandi was now no longer an obscure little village but had become a place of pilgrimage for all those who sought 'the ultimate truth'. Rai Bular was sick and his condition was deteriorating rapidly. His last days were brightened a little by the presence of his beloved Nanak by his side. From Talwlandi, Nanak went to Sultanpur to meet his sister Nanki and her husband Jai Ram.

This marked the end of his second *udasi*.

Were there a kitchen square paved with gold
And of gold be the pots and pans,
Were the square be marked with silver lining
extending far
Were the water be from the Ganges
And the fire from the sacrificial yagna [ceremony]
Were the food be dipped in milk
And deliciously tender to the palate,
Of little account will all these be,
If the mind is absorbed in the True Name.

– *Raag Basant*[36]

Chapter 12

The Brahmin and His 'Kitchen'

The people of Sultanpur rejoiced on Nanak's return. They had all come to love him for his soft and gentle ways and to admire his honesty through the years that he had worked with Nawab Daulat Khan Lodhi. This affection was now tinged with respect because they had listened to, and had been impressed by, his sermons. Now, on his second visit, they turned up in increasing numbers to listen to him. They heard him carefully and then went home and sought to practise what they had learnt. It gave Nanak tremendous satisfaction to see the people of Sultanpur turning to the path of virtue and truth and leading honest and simple lives.

It was not long before restlessness came upon Nanak yet again for he felt that his mission still remained incomplete. Nanki, though saddened by her brother's decision, did not attempt to sway him from his call. But Nawab Daulat Khan Lodhi, when he heard of Nanak's decision to set forth once again, went to him and tried to persuade him to give up on his travels and settle down to preach the true path in Sultanpur.

'God knows your fame has spread far and wide in this area and there are many, many people who will seek to learn the word truth from you,' pointed out Daulat Khan.

'It is God's will that I must set out again. An inner voice summons me to set forth and it is a voice that will not be denied,' responded Nanak.

Nanak set forth again, this time towards the north. Before turning towards the mountains, he went first to the region between the rivers Ravi and Beas. On the banks of the Ravi, he found a piece of land where he decided to build his permanent home. One of Nanak's disciples, Ajit Randhawa of Pakhoke village, along with a group of other farmers, pledged this piece of land to Nanak and it was here that the foundations of a new settlement, Kartarpur (the abode of God) were laid.

However, this Kartarpur is not to be mistaken with the Kartarpur town that today flourishes about 15 km from Jalandhar in Punjab along the Sher Shah Suri Marg and is (or was till recently) known for its furniture business. This town was founded much later, in 1594, by the fifth Guru, Arjan Dev, on land granted during the reign of the third Mughal Emperor, Jalal-ud-din Muhammad Akbar, known popularly as Akbar.

Kartarpur, which Guru Nanak founded and where he breathed his last on 22 September 1539, is at a distance of 80 km from Lahore and 180 km from Nanakana Sahib (earlier called Talwandi) via Lahore and only about 2 km from the Indo–Pak border on the right bank of river Ravi. Nanak's shrine stands out as there is no habitation around. There is a nearby railway station which is named

The Brahmin and His 'Kitchen'

Darbar Sahib Kartarpur on the Lahore–Chak Amru line, in Shakkar Garh, district Narowal of West Punjab (now in Pakistan).

Once news of the new settlement spread far and wide, large groups of people of every faith and religion travelled to Kartarpur to pay their respects to the Guru and to seek his blessings. Kartarpur, like Talwandi and Sultanpur, soon took on the semblance of a pilgrim town. Before Nanak left on his third *udasi*, both his and Mardana's parents came and took up residence in Kartarpur.

Amongst the people who came to meet Nanak was a middle-aged Brahmin, who, from a young age, had been adopted by a swami in an ashram. The swami was a kind and patient teacher and, like the other children who had come to learn from him, the young Brahmin too had mastered the religious texts at a young age. The young Brahmin was amongst the brightest in his group and the apple of the swami's eye who saw a great future for the boy as a scholar and a religious leader, one who would blaze a new trail, and voiced this prediction on every possible occasion.

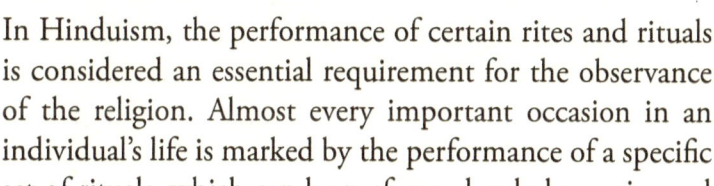

In Hinduism, the performance of certain rites and rituals is considered an essential requirement for the observance of the religion. Almost every important occasion in an individual's life is marked by the performance of a specific set of rituals, which can be performed only by a wise and learned Brahmin. As a result, in addition to the study of the holy texts the boys at the *gurukul*[37] also had to master the skill of performing these rituals correctly according to the strict parameters laid down by tradition.

The boy, now a young man, finished his studies, said goodbye to the swami and set out to make his mark in the world. He was a fine young man who possessed none of the arrogance that is the hallmark of most of the pandits and Brahmins who have mastered the religious texts and are looked upon as swamis by the people. Because of his mastery of the Hindu religious texts, he had established a name for himself which enabled him to give sound advice, both to the individuals, who came to him with their problems, and in his teachings.

If he ever gave any thought to this growing fame and popularity, he never allowed it to colour his speech or conduct. He remained humble and down to earth. He looked upon himself as a learner and never as a master. As a result, he gave thought to all shades of religious belief and practice, even if they were in direct conflict with his own.

In spite of this apparent mental flexibility, there was one thing on which he was completely rigid and inflexible – in the observance of rites and rituals. These had, over the years, become so deeply ingrained in his psyche that they were as essential a part of his life as the air he breathed.

Amongst other things, he also had a firm and strong belief in the caste system. Like all high-born Hindus, he was convinced that the caste we were born in was dictated by our deeds in our previous birth. People were born

The Brahmin and His 'Kitchen'

into high castes as a reward for the good deeds they had performed and into the low castes because of the sins they had committed in their previous birth. Surprisingly, despite being a kind and gentle human being for the most part, he did not extend any compassion to the unfortunate souls born in the low castes. He felt that they deserved the punishment they had been given for their past sins and it would only pollute the Brahmins if they came in touch with them.

In addition, the nature of the work they were called upon to perform – as scavengers, skinners of dead animals and lifters of night soil – added to their impurity and they were to be shunned at all costs. In spite of all his open-mindedness to other's ideas and his constant exposure to other sets of thoughts, this was one belief that remained strongly fixed in his mind and led him to go against his basic nature and be unkind to people belonging to the low castes. So afraid was he of being contaminated by the touch of a low-born, that he did not trust anyone to cook his food for him, and always cooked for himself.

The Brahmin found himself in the vicinity of the *dera* that was being built at Kartarpur. He had heard a great deal about Nanak: of his gentleness and simplicity and of the simple path to godliness that he preached. He was naturally curious about the new ideas concerning the practice of religion and had often wondered about the Guru and his teachings. Now that he found himself so close to the Guru's abode, his curiosity was whetted beyond containment and he could not keep himself from going out to meet him.

Nanak, as was his wont, welcomed him with open arms. Over the years, he had heard good things about the Brahmin and he too looked forward to the exchange of ideas that would occur through this interaction. Nanak sent for some water and personally poured it for the Brahmin so that he could wash his dust-covered hands, face and feet.

'Come, come my friend and be comfortable.' Nanak settled his guest on a wooden bed and placed bolsters behind his back to add to his comfort. An attendant brought a glass of water for the guest. The Brahmin peered suspiciously into his face and then waved him away.

'Thank you,' he said to Nanak. 'But I am not in the least thirsty.'

Nanak smiled to himself. He had met enough caste-conscious Brahmins in his life and understood the true reason for the Brahmin's refusal. After spending a few minutes in exchanging pleasantries, Nanak said: 'You must be tired and hungry after your long journey. Let us go and partake of the *langar* [community meal] and then you can rest for a while.'

The Brahmin recoiled from this suggestion, his face showing clearly the abhorrence that he felt. The ground on which the cooking fires had been lit would not have been consecrated according to the proper rituals and God alone knew what caste the cooks belonged to – heaven forbid, one of them might even be an untouchable. No, he could not bring himself to eat in the *langar*.

He looked up and saw Nanak waiting for him, a gentle smile playing at the corner of his lips. The Brahmin was

The Brahmin and His 'Kitchen'

sure that Nanak understood his predicament and if he gave voice to it, would not insist that he eat in the *langar*.

'I only eat what I have cooked myself. It is a practice that I have followed since I was little more than a child. And I only build my hearth on ground that has been duly consecrated,' the Brahmin said.

'Then we must not make a break with this practice. I would not cause discomfort to a guest at any cost. Tell me what you need in order to be able to cook your meal and it will be arranged.'

He was provided everything that he asked for: digging implements, holy water from the river Ganga, new cooking utensils, firewood and the provisions for his meal. Nanak watched intently as the Brahman marked a square in the ground and began to dig it up.

'What are you doing?'

'I am digging a cubit of earth.'

'And why do you do this?'

'I am doing this to ensure that this particular piece of ground has not been used for burial.'

Even as he spoke, his pickaxe turned up a few bones. The Brahmin recoiled in horror, abandoned his digging of the square and turned to mark a new square.

'I can understand your need to ensure that your cooking area is clean and pure and has never been used as a burial or funeral ground. But how can you ensure this by digging up the earth? All that your digging will do is turn up Muslim bones, because the Muslims alone bury their dead. How can you be sure, even in the absence of any bones, that this particular square of land has not been used for the cremation of a Hindu?' asked Nanak.

It was simple logic, but it was irrefutable and the Brahmin was left with no answer.

Nanak continued speaking: 'I saw the way you turned the glass of water away. And I know it is because you were afraid that the person serving you might be an untouchable. Your refusal to eat food cooked by another also stems from your fear of being contaminated by eating food cooked by a person from the low caste.'

Though he did not look at Nanak, the Brahmin nodded his head in agreement.

Nanak spoke further: 'Though you shun all contact with the low caste, you do not hesitate to use him [a low-caste member] in every way you can. When his shadow falls on you, you become impure and as part of your purification ritual, you bathe with the very water that he carries from the well for you every morning. You do not want him to cook your food because you will be contaminated, but you cook the very grain that he has raised through his labour in your fields. If by letting his shadow fall across you and by eating the food that he has cooked you are contaminated, then how do you justify bathing with the water that he has drawn and carried and cooking the food that he has grown? This will have rendered you impure already.'

Once again it was simple but irrefutable logic and once again the Brahmin had no answer.

Nanak put a gentle hand on his guest's shoulder and said: 'In the eyes of God we are all one. A man's place in the world and in life does not depend on the accident of

The Brahmin and His 'Kitchen'

his birth but on the actions that he performs and how these impact the lives of the people around him. A person born into a so-called low caste, who performs good deeds all his life and thinks always of the welfare of those around him, is definitely a better person than someone born into a so-called high caste, who spends his life indulging in selfish pleasures and performing deeds that bring no good to the community. It is not the external consecration or purification of the body or the kitchen square that is important, but the internal consecration of the spirit and the soul.'

After a long moment of silence, the Brahmin looked up into Nanak's face and smiled and said: 'I am starving. Can we please go and partake of the *langar*?'

The Brahmin came to blaze a trail that no one else had before him. He preached not only the Hindu religious thought, the way of life that the Vedas, the Upanishads, the Gita and the other holy texts taught but also against the practice of empty meaningless rituals.

He who labours, earns and gives in charity,
Says Nanak, he has understood the Truthful one.

Shloka[38]

Chapter 13

THE JOY OF GIVING

AFTER SPENDING A FEW MONTHS IN KARTARPUR, NANAK resumed his third journey.

He and Mardana had spent a lifetime on the road and had now got accustomed, not only to the long and weary hours of walking but also to the incidental discomforts of inclement weather, having sometimes to go without food and a proper shelter at night, though, rarely, a hostile welcome from the people they met on the way. Nanak's fame had spread far and wide and he was recognized as a holy man who preached a new and different path to God and godliness. Everywhere he went people ran out to welcome him and gathered in clusters to hear his teachings. They willingly brought whatever they could for the evening *langar* and vied with each other to be of service to the Guru.

Of course, there were still those who resented him and the message that he preached. Fundamentalist *maulvis* (Islamic scholars) and orthodox pandits all mocked him and took every opportunity to try and establish that he was no more than a charlatan who sought to exploit the simple, gullible working men and women. Those with money and power were not all like Duni Chand and Malik Bhago, ready to understand the lessons that the Guru taught and to make them an integral part of their lives.

There were many who resented not only Nanak's preaching that all human beings were equal but also his attempts to create a casteless society and his propagation of the view that God judged human beings not by their birth, the wealth that they accumulated or the company they kept, but by their actions. They saw in this philosophy the seeds of their own undoing and the loss of the absolute hold that they had held on poor people for centuries. They too did whatever they could to make life uncomfortable for the sage. At first, they were openly rude and hostile often to the point of being abusive. Through it all he remained always his serene, calm self and never showed any signs of anger or hatred towards those who wished him harm, winning great admiration in the process.

One evening, Nanak and Mardana reached a setting so perfect that it seemed to have been created specially for them. There was a bowl-shaped depression in the ground, one side of which was enclosed by a small group of huts belonging to the cowherd community. A little further, they could see a prosperous settlement. There was a river that encircled two sides of the bowl and then ran on towards the town, which was built in almost equal proportions, on either side of the river. The weather was mild and though the cowherds begged Nanak to make one of their huts his temporary home, Nanak chose to camp out in the open under a spreading *maulsari* (Spanish cherry) tree.

The Joy of Giving

The little community of cowherds had heard of Nanak and some were even familiar with his Bani. They did everything within their means to make their revered guest feel comfortable. Word spread quickly about his presence and, as the evening shadows lengthened, people from the town came to pay their respects to this most holy of men. In the days that followed, the crowd that came to join in Nanak's satsang gradually swelled. By the end of the week it appeared that the entire community had committed itself to making Nanak's visit a grand success. Everyone who came tended to linger on in the serene and picturesque atmosphere of the surroundings, which served as a perfect background to Nanak's sermons and to the singing and recitation of his Bani.

Nanak had made a deep impression upon the people with his hymns, his simple way of life and the sagacious words of wisdom that he spoke to the gatherings, which grew till every man and woman and child of the area came regularly to listen to him ... everyone, except the richest and the most powerful man in town.

No one called him by his real name and, if truth be told, there were many in the town who did not even know what his real name was. He was always addressed and spoken of simply as 'Karori' – someone whose wealth ran into crores. He did not take exception to the nickname and was even secretly pleased by it.

Karori had everything that a man could desire: wealth beyond measure, a palatial home, a beautiful wife and children. He dressed in the richest of clothes and ate the choicest of foods. He had faithful and devoted servants at his beck and call who anticipated his every need and hurried to meet it even before he could give voice to it. There was nothing more that Karori could possibly want or desire and he was the envy of all who knew him.

However, Karori had a troublesome secret: he could not get a good night's rest. He would toss and turn, and sleep would come to him only in fitful snatches and that too would be rudely disturbed by nightmares. He could no longer digest the tasty dishes, which he once so relished.

Karori's wife was extremely regular in her attendance at Nanak's satsangs and the effect of these visits was soon there for all to see. Her face was radiant as it had never been before and everything in her words and her mien spoke of being at peace with the world and herself. Karori envied her new-found happiness and serenity. One evening, when she returned home from the satsang, he gave voice to his envy.

'Then why don't you too come with me?' she asked.

'I don't come with you because your Nanak cannot help me. What relief can a purveyor of mere words bring when the most learned of physicians have failed? He is no healer and I have seen enough of so-called holy men and faqirs to have anything but the strongest contempt for them,' responded Karori.

In spite of his strong reservations, when a few more days elapsed with no abating of the deep and abiding joy on his wife's face, curiosity got the better of him and, putting aside his prejudices, he accompanied her to the satsang.

Soon he became like his wife a regular at the satsangs. He was drawn to Nanak's radiant presence and his divine words and began to linger on long after the satsang was over, till one day he and his wife were the last two disciples left in Nanak's presence.

The sun had set. Darkness had started gathering and little twinkling lights had begun to come on in the town, half-a-mile away from Nanak's camp. Nanak smiled at Karori, who even in the gathering gloom felt the warmth and radiance of that smile. Nanak beckoned the couple to come closer to him.

'Something weighs upon your mind, my friend: one requires no powers of clairvoyance to discern that you are a troubled man. Tell me your troubles, perhaps I may be able to help. If not, the mere telling may lighten your burden,' said Nanak.

Karori told Nanak of his troubles and Nanak listened attentively. When he had finished, Nanak put his hand lightly on Karori's shoulder and said: 'There is little that I can do or say to bring you relief. But there is something that you can do to help me.'

Karori exchanged a brief glance with his wife, as much as to say: 'See. Didn't I tell you? What good can a faqir be to me? Here he is burdening me with his own problem instead of offering me any help with mine.'

Nanak caught that look and understood the import of it. But he held his peace and went on with his request: 'Even though your town is prosperous, there are many residents who are very poor. They come to attend my satsang and look forward to the free meal that the langar provides. For some, this is the only real nourishment that they get during the day. Could you find it in your heart to set up a community kitchen for the poor and provide them with two simple meals a day? I ask this of you because I know you are the only one with the means for doing this.'

Nanak's last remark filled Karori with pride. Not for nothing was he known as Karori. His head teemed with ideas and, over the next few days, all his energies and his thoughts were focused on his kitchen alone. So preoccupied was he that he did not notice that he was eating and sleeping better. Karori personally supervised the cooking and the distribution of the food. Within a week, he had come to know all the indigent people who came to eat in the kitchen. For the first time in his life, he saw them as individual human beings and found himself being drawn into their lives and becoming aware of their many problems and worries. Some had medical problems; some others were involved in land disputes, while a few others struggled for a roof over their heads. The list of problems grew longer with each passing day and Karori found himself involved more and more in trying to resolve them.

In addition to his kitchen, he set up a dispensary and a school where the poorest of the poor children, instead of paying a fee, received a stipend for attending school. Those who were homeless were provided assistance, both financial and otherwise, to build themselves a simple home. He would return home late at night, weary and exhausted and, after a hearty meal, would fall immediately into a deep and untroubled sleep. He did attend Nanak's satsangs as regularly as he could but his preoccupation with his projects precluded his spending as much time as he would have wished to with his Guru.

One day, he heard that the Guru would be moving on in a few days and so, putting all his work aside, he went to meet Nanak. Nanak smiled at him indulgently.

'Come *bhai* Karori. Come and sit beside me and tell me more about your indigestion and your insomnia,' said Guru Nanak.

Karori knew that the Guru was teasing him and replied: 'There has been a miracle master. Thanks to you, my insomnia and lack of appetite have both vanished.'

To this, Nanak replied: 'I only gave you the prescription; you worked out the cure yourself. In any case, both you and I know that there is no such thing as a miracle. Your insomnia and your loss of appetite were both caused by your attitude and your way of life. Your lack of concern for those around you affected your sleep and your health. Once you started your community kitchen, you discovered the great joy that is to be obtained from giving and sharing. Your concern is now no longer only for yourself but also for others. Your obsession is no longer with merely amassing wealth but also with the happiness that your wealth can bring to others. You have subjugated the self to the service of mankind and, as a result, you have attained a state of bliss that few achieve. You are now a true man of God.'

He continued to be called Karori, but now when people used this name they did not mean a man who possessed crores; he was now Karori because he donated in crores.

Nanak trekked north from Sialkot through the lower mountain ranges of Jammu and into the Kashmir Valley. He met groups of pilgrims on their way to the holy shrine of Amarnath[39] and preached the concept of one supreme God and the path that could be followed in His search.

He trekked through difficult mountain regions, crossing many high ranges till he came to Sumeru, the legendary Mount Kailash.[40] During this difficult and arduous trek, Nanak crossed the Zoji-la pass into Ladakh. It seems that he followed the course of the upper Indus. This stretch of his journey brought him into contact with a group of Siddhas or perfect yogis and the Janamsakhis give us details of the discussions that took place and how Nanak finally won over the Siddha community and showed them the true path.

During this *udasi*, Nanak is also believed to have travelled through Nepal and Sikkim and also through Tibet. He returned to Sialkot through the hills of Kashmir.

There is one God
He is the supreme truth.
He the creator
Is without fear and without hate.
He the omnipresent
Pervades the universe.

– *Mool Mantra*[41]

Chapter 14

THE ABODE OF GOD

GREAT WAS THE JOY IN NANKI AND JAI RAM'S HEARTS on the return of their beloved Nanak. The people of Sultanpur celebrated the return of their most celebrated son by lighting up the town with thousands of oil lamps and emblazoning the sky with the many coloured flares of fireworks. It seemed as if Diwali was being celebrated on the return of Ram and Sita after their fourteen-year-long exile.

For many days thereafter, Sultanpur was witness to the arrival and departure of *jathas* (groups) of Nanak's disciples from nearby towns and villages who jostled for their Guru's glimpse and blessings. Gradually, the excitement died down and the town returned to its normal day-to-day routine and Nanki was glad to have her brother to herself. But this was not to be for long. Once Nanak felt rested both in body and mind, he had the same restless urge of the spirit come upon him once again. Yet again, the conviction grew that his mission was not quite complete. He had undertaken several journeys to take his message to the eastern, southern and the northern corners of India. However, he still had not made a trip to the west.

As Nanak set about making his preparations, Nanki felt that her heart would burst if her beloved brother were to go away again as she would not be able to bear his absence yet again. For once, she begged him to stay a few more days and Nanak, looking into her careworn face, lived through all the memories of her great love for him, and could not say no and agreed to defer his departure.

It was just as well that he did, for, a few days later, Nanki came down with a mysterious ailment and breathed her last in 1518 at the age of fifty-four. Three days later, Jai Ram, not able to sustain the loss, also passed away. There was nothing now to hold Nanak back and he made his preparations to leave in right earnest.

Shortly before Nanak left, Daulat Khan, who was at that time making his bid for the throne in Delhi, came to see him and tried one last time to persuade him to give up his travels. This was to be their last meeting.

Nanak, accompanied by the ever faithful Mardana, first travelled north to Multan and then to Sukkur from where he turned southwards along the river Indus till he reached Thatta (now in Sindh). From here he went west to Hinglaj (now in Balochistan), where he met a group of pilgrims who had embarked on the Haj – a pilgrimage to the holy Islamic cities of Mecca and Medina that all true Muslims are enjoined upon to perform at least once in their lifetime. He joined the group and crossed the Arabian Sea with them.

Nanak was dressed in blue robes, a colour considered sacred by the Muslims and favoured by their holy men. He also carried all that a pilgrim to the holy city of Mecca

The Abode of God

carries: a staff, a prayer mat, the holy book Quran and a pot for his morning ablutions. The boat that had carried them across the Arabian Sea brought them to Jeddah and the pilgrims joined a caravan on its way to Mecca.

Soon they were joined by many other caravans. Though these caravans travelled together across the desert, they kept their separate identity. When they camped at night, the tents of each caravan were clustered together but a distance was also maintained between them. Similarly, each caravan lit its own cooking fire and did not share it with the others. These cooking fires also served the purpose of keeping the travellers warm against the cold of the desert night.

Every evening, before the travellers got ready to sleep, Nanak sat outside his tent talking to all who would listen to him and explained the simple basic precepts of the new religious philosophy that he was propagating. Some, who were suspicious, kept away from him. Others listened to him and understood that all he was saying was that true religion meant living a simple, honest life in which we help others and try not to hurt anyone. He was showing them the way to being good human beings.

They reached a little habitation on the outskirts of Mecca, from where each caravan went its separate way. Nanak found the place so peaceful that he decided to tarry here for a few days before taking the final step to Mecca. The pilgrims bade him farewell with heavy hearts, for over those long days of tiresome journey, they had been touched by his gentleness and his unflagging cheerfulness, which lightened their darkest and most weary moments.

He stood under a tree watching them go. Then he turned to Mardana and the two set out to find a place where they could rest for the night. They found the place soon enough. It was a beautiful little mosque built on a raised platform and, beside it, there was an old tree. As they walked past it they were greeted by the *maulvi*, who, having finished with the evening prayers, sat on the doorstep of the mosque savouring the cool breeze of the evening.

'Greetings,' he said kindly. 'You look like you are strangers to these parts.'

'Yes,' Nanak answered. 'We are travellers from Hindustan and have come to offer prayers at the holiest of holy shrines in Mecca.'

'So are you pilgrims performing the Haj?' the *maulvi* asked Nanak.

Nanak shook his head.

'No, we are not pilgrims because we are not Muslims.'

The *maulvi* stared at them. There was nothing in the holy book which said that a non-Muslim could not make the pilgrimage to Mecca. But he had never heard of such a thing happening before and he felt the stirring of a deep admiration for this stranger, who even though he was not a Muslim, had performed the long and arduous journey to reach the holy shrine.

'You are welcome to my humble abode and I will be honoured if you deign to be my guests,' said the *maulvi*.

'That we will do gladly,' Nanak replied. 'Such graciousness bears out what your beard and your robes proclaim: that you are a man of God.'

The *maulvi* led them into the one-room structure that stood to one side of the mosque. They took their shoes off at the door and sat down, cross-legged, on a faded, old carpet. He served them water followed by goat's milk in small earthen bowls.

Their conversation was at first formal and stilted, punctuated with long and frequent silences. But they soon found that they shared the same thoughts and beliefs about human conduct and, gradually, fell into ease with each other, till it seemed as if they had been friends all their lives.

A little later, a young man brought a tray of food for the *maulvi*.

'I do not need to cook my meals,' the *maulvi* explained. 'Members of the congregation take turns to send me food.'

He shared the meal that was meant only for him with Nanak and Mardana and that one helping of food was more than enough to feed the three of them.

By now, darkness had gathered around them and, yet, they sat by the light of a small lamp, talking late into the night. At last, they knew that even though they did not want to pause in their discussion, pause they must because it was time to go to bed. Each of them drew his covering over himself. After that, the *maulvi* snuffed out the lamp and, after exchanging good nights, they drifted off to sleep. Nanak awoke a short while later, with a feeling of discomfort. The room was small, meant only for one occupant and, though the little window and the door were wide open, it had become stuffy. As he lay awake in the dark staring at the ceiling, he could sense the restless turning of the other two and knew that they too were troubled by the stuffiness of the room.

He stole quietly out of the room. Outside, the moon shone in all its glory and touched everything around with a touch of silver. Nanak found a place at the edge of the platform where he would not be under the shade of the tree, and, drawing his shawl around him, he was soon fast asleep. The night breeze struck up soon after. But Nanak, weary and exhausted after the long days of travelling, had fallen into a deep slumber and did not feel its chill. When, in the early dawn, the *muezzin* at the mosque gave his call for the morning prayer (*azaan*), all that Nanak did was to draw his chaddar closer around his head and curl up a little more, as if to shut out the sound.

As the congregation scattered after the prayers, a few curious ones lingered on to stare at the man who had slept all through the *azaan* and the *faj'r* (the morning namaz).

Then one of them pointed at his feet and said loudly, 'Look, look. His feet are pointing towards the Kaaba.'

The others looked towards Nanak's feet. Yes, they were pointing towards the Kaaba, the holiest and most revered shrine of the Muslims. They began to murmur among themselves and a few of them ran off to call the other members of the congregation who had not noticed this terrible act of sacrilege. Knowing the mildness of their *maulvi*, and fearing that he would not mete out a severe enough punishment to the kafir (infidel), one of them ran off to find Qazi Rukn-ud-din (who was a strict follower of Islam). The hostile murmur grew louder and louder and the *maulvi*, who was still inside the mosque, came out to see what the clamour was all about.

'Look, look *maulvi sahib*. This infidel has his feet pointing towards the Kaaba. You must punish him,' insisted one of the onlookers.

The *maulvi* knew that the members of his congregation were overreacting. After their long discussion of the night before, he knew that Nanak would never dream of hurting anyone's religious sentiments, no matter which religion they belonged to. He had come out in the dark and had unwittingly lain down in a position that pointed his feet towards the Kaaba. He shook Nanak awake. Nanak sat up, his shawl falling away from his head and shoulders. He looked up at the scowling faces of those who stood crowding around him and then he looked into the *maulvi's* gentle face.

'What is it?' Nanak asked. 'What have I done to cause so much anger?'

'You slept with your feet pointing towards the Kaaba,' the *maulvi's* voice was gentle but this only served to anger the fanatics even more. By now, the *qazi* had arrived on the scene and his anger at the sin that the kafir had committed was terrible to behold. He struck Nanak on his legs with his staff half-a-dozen times.

'What you have done is truly terrible: you have pointed your feet at the abode of God. It is obvious that you are a kafir. But this is so great an act of sacrilege that you deserve severe punishment for it. As your first act of atonement and repentance you must rub your face with ash and beg for forgiveness,' declared the *qazi*.

'I deserve your censure, just as I deserve any punishment that you might give me. I have indeed insulted God. But I am a poor ignorant fool and know so little. Could you help me please by pointing my feet towards a place where God does not reside?'

The *maulvi* realized instantly what Nanak was trying to tell the gathering and smiled to himself, though he took care to turn his face away from the *qazi* so that the stern, rigid man would not see him smile. Two youngsters ran forward and picked up Nanak's legs by the feet but as they swung them away from the direction of the Kaaba, they suddenly paused; the full import of Nanak's words finally hit them. Where was there a place in this world where God did not reside? They looked to the qazi for directions. Rigid and fanatical as he was, the *qazi* knew there was no refuting the point that Nanak had made. God was omnipresent. No matter in which direction they turned Nanak's feet God would be found there. Nanak smiled gently at the confusion that showed clearly on the young men's faces.

Nanak turned to the qazi and said: 'Forgive me your holiness. All my life I have been taught that God is omniscient and omnipresent, that he is all-pervading and all-seeing; that he lives in the clouds and the stars and the moon and the sun; that his spirit breathes in the breeze that blows and in the rain that falls; that he lives even within all of us. The structures that we make and revere, the mosques and the temples and, yes, even the holiest of the holy, the Kaaba, are meant to draw men together in congregational prayers and to focus our thoughts on

God. Over the years, they become the repositories of the prayers of the thousands of worshippers who throng them and hence attain a measure of divinity. But in spite of this, they cannot contain and limit the spirit of God and fool us into thinking that they alone are the abode of God. Tell me your holiness, are the beliefs and teachings of your religion to the contrary?'

The *qazi* stood in silence for a while, too amazed to look Nanak in the eye. But he was, in spite of his sternness and rigidity, a good and fair man. He took control of his thoughts and looked up at last into Nanak's eyes.

'You have shamed me in my rigid and orthodox thoughts. You are right: God lives everywhere, in every leaf that flutters in the trees,' he said looking up at the tree as a sudden gust of wind blew through its branches. 'He lives in our hearts and minds. And his temple and his abode are everywhere.'

Nanak lived with the *maulvi* in his little home for a number of days and, every day, the *qazi* came to see him and involved him in discussions on many theosophical issues. Seeing their religious leader paying so much attention to the holy man they had once considered a kafir, the people of the habitation too came to listen to Nanak. They soon discovered that there was a great deal that was common between their religion and what the holy man preached and this won their trust and they listened to Nanak with greater attention and respect.

The *maulvi* had become a disciple in every respect and the *qazi* had become a true friend. When it was time for Nanak to leave they said their goodbyes with heavy hearts.

There was lightness in Nanak's step as he walked away with a song in his heart. His purpose in undertaking this long and arduous journey and coming so far away from home had been more than fulfilled.

God is great!
God is great!
There is no God
Except the one God.
Stand up for the good!
The timeless one is the Truth,
Submit to the Name,
Salutations to all.
The Lord is merciful.
He is the creator of all life.

– Nanak's *'azaan'*, from Bhai Mani Singh's Janamsakhis[42]

Chapter 15

MUSIC AND WORSHIP

𝓕ROM MECCA, NANAK AND MARDANA WENT ON TO THE holy city of Medina. After spending a few days there they travelled towards the north-east across the Arabian Desert till they reached Baghdad on the banks of the river Tigris.

The city of Baghdad, as we know it today, was founded in A.D. 769 on the site of an older city of the same name by Caliph Al-Mansur. It was designed to be the new capital of the Caliphate Empire. The caliph had chosen the site well. It had a mild, temperate climate and, topographically, offered easy possibilities of defence. It had proximity to water as it was built on the banks of the river Tigris and had access to the river Euphrates through a system of canals and bridges. But, most importantly, it was built on the Khurasan route, which was the meeting point of the caravans from the four cardinal directions and thus had easy access to every trading possibility. It was also an important stop for those making the sacred pilgrimage of Haj to the holy city of Mecca.

It was no wonder that soon after it was established, Baghdad became the focal point of the Islamic Golden Age. Because of its many attractions, more and more people chose to settle here and it soon became a hub for the pursuit of both knowledge and culture. The location of Baghdad was ideal for the production of paper and this, in turn, led to an ever-increasing production of books, which resulted in the mushrooming of bookstores and libraries. Schools for every conceivable discipline flourished and Baghdad became the centre of learning of the Islamic world. It is claimed that, in its heyday, Baghdad eclipsed even Ctesiphon, the capital of the Persian Empire in its glory.

Sadly, it lost its pre-eminence with the shifting of the capital to Samara. It suffered further when Halagu Khan, the Mongol chieftain, sacked it in 1258. Though it had lost its position of pre-eminence in the Islamic world, yet it continued to boast of at least a dozen famous schools of Islamic studies.

It was to this Baghdad that Nanak came. He set up camp in a tomb on the outskirts of the city. It was a simple, modest-sized one: built of undressed stone, set in the centre of a fair-sized courtyard, which, in turn, was enclosed by a stone wall with arched alcoves set in it. It was obviously the tomb of an important person, someone who either had power and position while he lived or someone who had been highly respected.

There were no attendants in residence and yet there was no air of neglect about the building. The premises were clean and wore an air of having been freshly swept, and over the grave, there were remnants of the Thursday evening prayers – little oil lamps and a fresh chaddar covering the grave. Obviously, someone still cared enough for the departed soul to offer prayers in his memory. Nanak felt a kinship with the air of calm and serenity that pervaded the structure and was happy with his choice of the camping site.

That evening, in the quiet, peaceful atmosphere of the tomb, Nanak decided to conduct his prayer meeting. When Mardana tuned his rabaab and struck up the accompaniment to his master's singing, two little heads appeared on top of the boundary wall and two sets of curious eyes peered down at the strangers. Two young boys playing outside the tomb had heard the strange and unusual sound of prayers in another language and then of the singing, and intrigued by them, had climbed onto the wall to investigate.

Once the prayers were over Nanak beckoned them to come and receive *prasad*. After an initial hesitation, the boys came into the courtyard. The ease with which they came, it was obvious that they were familiar with the place. The elder of the two looked up into Nanak's face and asked: 'Who are you?'

'We are travellers from Hindustan. We had come to

visit the holy cities of Mecca and Medina and are now on our way home,' replied Nanak.

The boys were quiet for a while and then it was the turn of the younger one to ask a question: 'What was it that you were singing?'

'We were singing a song in praise of the Supreme Being. Singing is an essential part of our worship,' explained Nanak.

The boys looked at each other and then the older one said: 'You must forgive us if we find your form of worship strange. Music does not form a part of our worship.'

The boys lingered on a while longer, intrigued by the strangers. Then, as the evening shadows lengthened and darkness began to gather, Nanak smiled at the two boys and said: 'It's getting late. You better go home or else your parents will begin to worry about you.'

The boys told a few of their friends about the strangers who had camped in the tomb and about their strange form of worship. On the second evening, a fairly large group had gathered in the tomb to listen to this strange man and his strange form of worship. When Nanak burst into a song, there was a moment of confused stillness. Some were touched by the beauty of the song; some did not know what to make of this strange form of worship, and there were still others who were angry and upset that one of the tenets of orthodox Islam, which forbade the use of music in worship, was being violated. But the predominant mood was one of confusion as to how to react to this strange and controversial practice. When Nanak finished his hymn, he greeted the group of people with a smile and with folded

Music and Worship

hands. A few answered his greetings but the majority slunk away guiltily, as if even by just listening to Nanak's song they would be committing a sin.

Word of the strange practice spread like wildfire through the town. The flames of anger and hostility were fanned by the custodians of the orthodox form of Islam, which was practised by the vast majority of the residents. This group had a fiery discussion about the sacrilege that the stranger had committed and how he must be punished. Members of this group fanned out into the more thickly inhabited localities of the town, where they described the terrible sin of the strange faqir and how it was their duty, as true Muslims, to punish him for it. It was agreed that the apt punishment was the traditionally Arab one – stoning unto death.

That evening, as Nanak launched into his Bani a large, hostile group of men crowded around him. As they listened to the hymn, there were some among the crowd who were touched not only by the beauty of the melody but also by the purity and sweetness of Nanak's voice. They felt their anger melt away and found themselves looking uncomfortably at the stones they carried in their hands. Surely such beautiful music could only be of divine origin and deserved to be rewarded rather then be punished. However, the mood among the majority remained hostile. This strange and forbidden form of worship was a threat to their religion and, if it was not nipped in the bud, it could grow in popularity and endanger the very existence of Islam.

The most potent force in uniting people and motivating them to violence is a perceived threat to their religion. The tendency towards violent action had gained such force in the minds of the mob that it was only a question of the first stone being thrown. But before one of the hot-headed, orthodox fundamentalists could take upon himself to cast the first stone, Nanak's hymn came to a close, and after a moment of silence, he surprised his listeners by breaking into the *azaan* that the *muezzin* sang each time he called the faithful to prayer. Beyond the opening lines, the words were strange, but there was no mistaking the melody.

They had heard the *azaan* a thousand times before, but there was something very special about this one. It was sweet and pure like the waters of a mountain spring and had the poignancy of the longing of a *murid* (a follower or a disciple) for his absent *murshid* (teacher) and the intensity of the desire of a dervish for his absent master. Paradoxically, it also had the peace and serenity of one who has been face to face with the Maker. The opening had echoed the *muezzin*'s call and the strange new words that came later only reiterated what Islam had taught them.

The *azaan* is considered by many, including non-Muslims, to be the most beautiful music in the world and Nanak's rendering bore this contention out in ample measure. The hearts of the listeners swelled with inexplicable happiness, a happiness so intense that it brought tears to their eyes. Even the most orthodox and hostile amongst the crowd were moved by the sheer beauty of Nanak's *azaan*. They knew that, in that moment, they had experienced divinity. As if on a pre-arranged signal, the stones dropped from their hands and as the singing finished, the fundamentalists fell as one on their knees, to pray.

Music and Worship

No words were said, no words needed to be said. Nanak had made his point. The Prophet Muhammad had banned the singing of songs, which could cause evil passions. The singing of the eulogies of God, like the *azaan*, however, was food for the soul.

Man comes as ordained by Him,
He goes under His command.
He leads a truthful life under the Absolute Guru
And the Word Divine makes him realise God's
grandeur and excellence.

– *Sidh Gosht,* 22[43]

Chapter 16

THE WIDOW AND HER LOST SON

*I*N A LITTLE SETTLEMENT ON THE BANKS OF THE TIGRIS, some distance from Baghdad, lived a fifty-year-old poor widow. Her husband had died when she was only twenty-five. It was true that he had not left her with any financial support, but then, as she was fond of saying, neither had he left her with any financial liabilities. He had, of course, left her with a five-year-old son who became the centre of her life. Everything she did centred around the little boy.

When a year after her husband's death, it had been suggested by the elders of the village that she marry again, she refused. They tried to counsel her that since she had a full life ahead of her and the added responsibility of bringing up her son, it would be easier for her if she had a husband to share her responsibilities.

She listened patiently. Then she shook her head and lapsed into a determined silence and nothing that the elders could say or do was able shake her from her conviction. One by one the elders left her little house.

Late one evening when the household chores were done, her neighbour came in to see her, as much to provide her with much-needed moral support as to hear all the gossip about the elders' visit.

'They talked great sense,' the neighbour said. 'This is the best course for you to adopt for yourself and your son.'

'It would seem so, because a home is never complete without a man,' agreed the widow. 'But show me the person, man or woman, who could love another's child as his own.'

The neighbour recognized the reference immediately. A few years ago, a widower of the village had married again in the hope that his new bride would be a mother to his two little children. As matters turned out, the 'witch' cast a spell on the man so that he had eyes and ears only for her, and persuaded him to pack the children off to their maternal grandparents. It was two years since this happened and the children had never been seen or heard of in the village again.

'You've got a point there,' the neighbour agreed. 'But life will be extremely difficult for you.'

'I will face all the difficulties with a smile if it ensures my son's happiness,' replied the widow.

In the years to come she remained true to her word. She struggled to earn enough money to keep body and soul together and to give her son a good upbringing. And, through these long difficult years, the smile never left her face. The son was as close to his mother as it is possible for a son to be. He returned his mother's love and devotion in more than ample measure. He worked diligently at his studies in the little school adjoining the *masjid* (mosque) run by a *maulvi* and was always ahead of the rest of the boys. In addition, within a few years of his father's death, he had started doing little chores for his neighbours in return for payment in cash or kind and so sought to lighten his mother's burden.

The boy grew into a handsome, strapping lad. He was intelligent, honest, hard-working and God-fearing and the envy of every other parent in the village. The other villagers never tired of remarking on how the widow, in her refusal to marry again, had made the right decision and were glad that her sacrifice had borne fruit in such generous measure.

As the boy grew into a young man, the widow wished him to get married so that she could have the comfort of ordering a daughter-in law about the house and the joy of dangling her grandchildren on her knee. But every time she broached the subject, he resolutely shook his head: 'Not till I have put away enough for your old age.'

In this resolve, she was reminded of the way she herself had turned down the advice of the elders all those long years ago and could not help but smile at the memory – he was, after all, her son.

When he was twenty, an offer came from his maternal uncle, who had only daughters, asking him to come and help him in his business. The widow was loath to let him go. But she was astute enough to know that this would perhaps be the only opportunity for him to get the economic security that he so desperately sought. Who knew, perhaps her brother would take such a liking to the boy that he would suggest that he marry one of his daughters. She felt a warm wave of happiness go through her at this prospect and she put all her doubts and hesitations aside and agreed to let him go.

They had lived a frugal life and their needs had always been very simple and basic. So, there was not much preparation to be made for the journey. As soon as they had enough money to cover the expenses, she gave him a small bundle containing some food and clothes and saw him off on the ferry that would take him across the river on the first leg of his journey. She stood on the bank, watching the boat pull away from the landing, muttering a prayer for her son's well-being. Then, unbelievable as it was, she saw the boat turn on its side and begin its descent to the bottom of the river. She stood there in a state of shock, watching the rescue attempts, watching the survivors being fished out of the water by the swimmers and divers who had rushed to the spot. Each survivor was handed over to the crowd on the landing and the rescue team went back to look for others. As time went on and fewer and fewer survivors were brought out of the water, the rescue operations seemed to loose their urgency.

Finally, they were given up altogether and the rescue boat returned to the shore. Friends and relatives crowded the landing and scanned the face of each survivor. Those who found their loved ones among the survivors heaved a sigh of relief, those who did not, felt their hearts sink a little and looked anxiously into the face of the next survivor. Finally, the last survivor was carried ashore. The widow stood on the river bank staring out at the waters, a long, long time and then turned and walked away. There was no sadness, no anxiety on her face, only a determined resolve.

Her neighbour, hearing of the tragedy, had rushed down to the river to be with her friend. But when she turned to offer her sympathies to the widow, her words were brushed aside: 'No, my son is alive. He will come back to me. Wait and see.'

This was her refrain in the days that followed. She had led a good, virtuous life and her son was a good, virtuous boy. God would never do this to them.

Over the next few days, the river yielded up some more of the dead, but her son was not amongst them and this only strengthened her conviction.

Her brother came to help with the funeral.

'No. My son is not dead,' she told him. 'He will come back to me. It is good of you to have come but there can be no funeral. There is no body and so my son is not dead.'

She clamped up after that and refused to say another word, rejecting all her brother's pleas. The *maulvi* came to reason with her but his efforts yielded similar results. Finally, the attempts to conduct a funeral were abandoned. The waters of time closed around the tragedy and life resumed its even course.

The brother suggested that she come with him and spend some time with his family. It would help to take her mind off her loss. But as far as she was concerned, there had been no loss.

'What will my son think when he returns and finds me gone?' the widow asked.

He had no reply to this question and, after offering her some financial help, he returned home.

The widow turned to faqirs and dervishes to find out when her son would return. She, who had had a good balanced head on her shoulders all these years, now abandoned all reason and fell prey to superstition. One faqir in particular had a strong appeal for her because he supported her in her belief that her son was alive and would return to her.

'A holy man will come from the east and he will restore your son to you,' the faqir had said to her.

This was all the assurance that she needed. Now, secure in her belief, she too resumed the even tempo of her life. The only departure was that, every evening, she would go down to the landing and stare longingly across the waters. Then she would sigh and return to the chore of cooking her evening meal.

Whenever there was news of a holy man on a visit to the area, she would rush to him to see if he was from the east. The answer would invariably be in the negative and she would return and resume the quiet routine of her life.

The days slipped past, sometimes with the speed of a few seconds, sometimes as if each day was a year. But she learnt to live with them all and waited, with monumental patience, for her holy man to appear.

It was now twelve long years since she had lost her son and she heard that another holy man had come and camped on the bank of the river. She ran to where he sat in the lotus position, his legs crossed. She sat at the edge of the crowd that pressed around him and looked closely at him. There was no questioning his divinity. The serenity of his face, the soft radiant smile playing on his lips, the gentleness of his words – all spoke of a highly evolved human being.

She did not want to disturb the holy man's sermon, but her curiosity could not be contained. She nudged her immediate neighbour and asked in a hushed whisper: 'Is he from the east?'

In an equally soft whisper her neighbour replied: 'Yes. They say he is from Hindostan.'

Her heart gave a lurch and she felt like picking her way through the crowd, throwing herself at his feet and asking him to bring back her son. Then she told herself that having waited patiently for twelve long years, she could surely wait for a few moments more, and held herself in check. So, she sat and listened to the holy man. But try as she would, her mind would not dwell on his words. All she could think of was the return of her son. Would he have changed beyond recognition over these twelve years or would he be the way he was when he went away? A hundred questions chased each other through her mind and a hundred plans were made for the future. The holy one finished his sermon and the listeners, one at a time, got up, touched his feet and walked away, silently pondering over the words that the stranger had spoken to them.

At last, when she was alone with the holy one, she could contain herself no longer. She got up, threw herself at Nanak's feet and began to weep. Nanak drew her up and wiped the tears from her eyes.

'Sit beside me mother and tell me the nature of your grief. I can see that you have waited a long time to be able to speak with me,' Nanak said.

His voice was the gentlest and the most comforting sound she had heard in her life.

'No,' she said, smiling through the residue of her tears. 'You can have no idea how long I have waited for you. It has been twelve years: twelve long years.'

Nanak waited for her to continue.

She got to her feet. 'Come,' she said, great urgency in her voice. 'Come with me.'

He too got to his feet and she led him to the landing where the boat had capsized all those years ago. She pointed to the jetty and began speaking: 'Twelve years ago I stood there watching the passengers climb into the ferry. Among them was my . . . son, going on a visit to his uncle, hoping for a better period in his life. This was the first time he was going away from me and, though my heart was heavy at his going, I knew that it was for his own good. He waved to me as the boat pushed away from the landing. Then as I watched, the boat suddenly capsized. The divers and the swimmers all climbed into a rescue boat and rowed quickly to the site of the accident to save as many people as they could. After a while, the rescue boat came back

The Widow and Her Lost Son

and berthed at the jetty and, as each survivor was handed up to the crowd, I scanned each face. But my son was not amongst them. Twenty-three people, including my son, never returned.'

She paused for breath and Nanak waited for her to finish her story.

She explained her situation to Nanak by saying: 'Then I met a faqir who told me that my son was alive and that a holy man from the east would bring him back to me. That night I had a dream. I saw a holy man. He was bathed in so radiant a light that I had to shield my eyes to be able to look at him. And even then I could not look him in the face. I did not then know who it was, but I know now that it was you. You held up your hand and a ray of light shone upon me: a light that filled my entire being with soft, glowing warmth. All sorrow left me and a voice whispered what the faqir had already said to me, that a holy man would come from the east and restore my son to me.'

She paused again and, now when she spoke, the quiver had miraculously left her voice and a radiant happiness had replaced the poignancy on her face.

'And now, here you are. I have always known that my son will come back to me. Today, I am more certain of it than ever before.'

Nanak was moved by the intensity of the woman's faith. 'Where do you think your son has been these last twelve years?' Nanak asked.

'Why, in the custody of Allah. Where else could he be! And He has kept him safe and well so that he could return to me,' the widow replied.

'And,' Nanak asked, his voice still quiet and gentle: 'Do you think that he has been happy while in Allah's custody?'

'Oh yes,' the woman said, her face lighting up with the thought of how her son had been while with Allah. 'He has known happiness unsullied by the shadow of grief and anxiety; unclouded by failure, frustration and betrayal; a happiness unknown to any mortal.'

There was not a shadow of doubt in her voice and Nanak knew that she believed implicitly in what she said.

'And you would be selfish enough to bring him back to this world where not a day passes without grief and sadness in some form or the other. You would wish to bring him back to a world where happiness is just an occasional episode in a long drama of pain and suffering?' Nanak asked.

The woman was silent, musing over Nanak's words. Nanak looked steadily into her eyes and putting his hand on her shoulder, squeezed it gently.

'Have you really lived without your son these last twelve years? I can see him in your eyes even now. I can see that in all these long years there was not a moment when he was not with you. Memories of his goodness and kindness to others made you smile and you cried bitter tears when you remembered the times of his pain. You gave him so much love when he was with you in flesh and blood that he can never really go away from you,' stated Nanak.

He could see the light return to those tired old eyes. 'You have not lost your son; you have only lost his body. His spirit and his soul will always remain with you, in all their strength and glory and will be with you till your dying day,' went on Nanak.

He paused and the widow looked steadily into his eyes. He then observed: 'Little mother, birth and death are not of our choosing. We come when God wills it and we go when He so desires. We cannot change this. No force on earth can change this. All that we can hope to do is to accept them both as two sides of his will and learn to live with the sorrow of death as easily as we live with the joy of birth.'

He paused for a while and then went on: 'While we live, we should endeavour to perform only good deeds and so ensure that we live on in the minds of others after we are gone, the way your son still lives on in your mind even after twelve long years.'

Realization dawned on the widow and she wept for the truth that the Guru had enabled her at last to perceive.

When her weeping was done, she touched the Guru's feet and turned and walked towards her hut. At last, she was at peace with herself, with the world and with God's will. Nanak had, indeed, given her son back to her.

In the days that followed, the number of people who came to listen to Nanak increased rapidly. They were more than a little reassured to find that there was nothing in what he said and preached that could be interpreted as a criticism of Islam. In fact, they were pleasantly surprised to find that there was a great deal in common in their own beliefs and in Nanak's teachings.

After some time, Nanak resumed his return journey to Kartarpur. From Baghdad he took the north-eastern route to Iran. He visited Kabul before reaching Peshawar. He passed through Kandahar (Afghanistan) and Hasan Abdal (Pakistan). After that, followed a south-eastern route to the Punjab. Mardana and he visited the shrines of Tilla Balnath and Katasraj (both now in Pakistan). From here they came to Saidpur, where one of Nanak's first disciples Lalo resided.

Unfortunately, their arrival in Saidpur coincided with the Mughal Emperor Babur's third incursion into India. Sialkot had offered no resistance and had been spared the usual bloody massacre and plunder. But Saidpur had offered resistance and, when it was finally captured, faced the full wrath of the conqueror. The soldiers were killed mercilessly, the civilian inhabitants were either sold into slavery or held captive and everything that could be plundered was seized by the conquering army.

Nanak was witness to this bloodthirsty treatment of the inhabitants of Saidpur and legend has it that he and Mardana too were taken prisoner. But then Babar heard of the strange faqir, whom even the Mughal guards had come to admire, and came down to pay the Guru a visit. It is said that he was so impressed by Nanak's speech, his obvious proximity to God and the divinity that coloured all his actions that he immediately ordered he be released and offered to give him whatever he wanted. Nanak asked for the release of all the inhabitants of Saidpur who had been taken prisoners. Not only did Babar accede to this request but he also returned all the property that had been confiscated and paid compensation for all that had been looted.

The heart-rending scenes that Nanak had witnessed at Saidpur moved him to compose hymns of the greatest poignancy and these hymns find pride of place in the Adi Granth.

Finally Nanak reached Kartarpur, which marked the end of his fourth and last *udasi*. His journeys had finally come to an end.

Like birds flocking to the trees at night,
Men cometh into this world.
Some repose in peace while others abide in distress.
Their eyes wander across the skies,
And they roam ceaselessly caught in the cycle of their deed.
Those joined to the Name regard this world
As the grazier's hut in the rain-grown pasture,
And they overcome their passion and anger ...

— *Raag Gauri*[44]

Chapter 17

MOOLA KEER AND THE JEWEL THIEF

*N*ANAK HAD FINALLY COME HOME.

Kartarpur had by now grown into a full-fledged township. Immediately after his arrival, Nanak laid aside the pilgrim's clothes that he had worn during his *udasis* and assumed the garb of an ordinary householder. He established a routine, which emphasized that the people living in Kartarpur were by no means members of a religious or monastic order, who had renounced the everyday world and were involved exclusively in the pursuit of religion and metaphysical thought. Each member of the community went about his or her ordinary, everyday occupation like all other normal people.

There was a great diversity of people, from different social backgrounds, different economic strata of society and different castes and creeds who came to live in Kartarpur and they were bound together by their faith in the Guru's teachings. They were drawn to Kartarpur by his message of piety, equality, compassion, charity, truth and truthful living.

Nanak had preached from the very beginning, that, in order to reap the fruits of a religious life, it was not necessary to renounce the world, go into isolated meditation in caves in the faraway Himalayas or to practise an elaborate code of conduct involving complicated rites and rituals. True religious discipline could only be achieved while living in the world of ordinary human beings, while coping with all its temptations and challenges, its joys and sorrows. All through his *udasis*, this had been the refrain of his discussions with the various groups of ascetics, yogis and *siddhas* (ascetics who have achieved enlightenment) who he had come into contact with.

Now, in his community in Kartarpur, this ideal was given practical shape. Members of the community lived in the material world with all its pitfalls and difficulties and yet strove to be kind, truthful, compassionate, honest and God-fearing.

The three great traditions that were established in Kartarpur were the traditions of *seva* or selfless service, *kirtan* or religious singing and *langar* or free kitchen.

Nanak had been practising the tradition of singing or recitation of the Bani, even before his enlightenment, in the form of the spontaneous composition of spiritually inclined poems. After his enlightenment, the singing of the Bani became integral to worship. Unlike the singing of bhajans by the Hindus, which was an accompaniment to their sermons or the reading from their holy texts, Nanak's sermon was his Bani. Whatever he wanted to preach was couched in its words, which came to him in the form of spontaneously inspired verse. This is why he would often turn to Mardana and say, 'Mardana, *Bani aaye hai* – I have inspiration for a Bani.' This would be the signal for Mardana to take up his rabaab and provide an accompaniment for the divinely inspired verses that Nanak sang. It was only when he was amongst strangers, who might not understand the language of his Bani, that Nanak would offer an exposition of what he had sung.

The Guru's compositions were sung at the appropriate times of the day to the accompaniment of Mardana's rabaab. This made the congregation familiar with the Guru's words. It also made the members of the congregation turn inwards into themselves and contemplate God's name.

During the most difficult days of his *udasis*, he sought, whenever he could, to get the *sangat* (the assembly of devotees and disciples) to organize a *langar* where the congregation would not only work together but also eat together. In Kartarpur, these traditions became firmly entrenched in the daily life of the community.

The *langar*, where all the members of the community ate together, not only served to remind his followers that the distinctions of caste, religion and social standing that Nanak so abhorred, were man-made and against the will of God, but also nurtured in the hearts of the members of the community, the desire for *seva*, or selfless service to the community. Everyone in Kartarpur, whoever could do so, involved himself or herself in the running of the *langar* in one way or the other. Water was drawn from the wells, the wheat was ground into flour, wood for the cooking fires was collected, the food was cooked and served and the used utensils were scrubbed clean. The *langar* came to foster the spirit of equality, humility and brotherhood amongst Nanak's disciples.

In addition to the original inhabitants of Kartarpur, who had come and settled here, when the Guru had first earmarked the site as his permanent home, there were now new settlers. Nanak's fame had spread far and wide and there were communities of his followers all along the routes that he had followed on his *udasis*. Groups of these people now wound their way to Kartarpur to pay homage to their Guru and to seek his blessings. Many of those who came were so impressed by the serene atmosphere that pervaded the settlement that they abandoned their homes and made new homes here.

One of the earliest settlers in Kartarpur was a trader by the name of Moola Keer. He was a wealthy man, but honest and God-fearing, always ready to lend a helping hand to others. All through the long years of Nanak's absence on his *udasis*, Moola Keer had gone out of his way to help new settlers find their feet in the settlement. As a result, he was extremely popular with the settlers and was highly respected. He had business interests in nearby towns as well and, through the contacts he had thus established, was able to provide help to the settlers.

He lived in a large and comfortable house to which he welcomed all with equal warmth. Soon it became an established fact that even total strangers, if they failed to find suitable accommodation elsewhere in Kartarpur, would be made more than welcome by Moola in his home. Though he was an extremely wealthy man, he lived a simple life and did not make any ostentatious display of his wealth. He dressed simply, in ordinary everyday clothes, ate simple wholesome food and gave generously to various charitable causes.

Having lived under the guidance of Nanak's teachings and having seen, over a period of time, the transformation they had wrought in all those who came to Kartarpur, Moola Keer was convinced that anyone who was a disciple of Nanak was bound to be a good, virtuous human being, a role model for others. To some extent, this conviction was justified, because Nanak's disciples conducted themselves with such dignity and decorum and displayed such a strong and unswerving sense of right and wrong, that they were regarded with respect and a little awe by everyone else.

Moola Keer had an attractive, loving wife. She was in every way an equal partner to her husband's goodliness – warm-hearted and generous, who always helped others. If there was one weakness she had, it was her love for jewellery. Moola had at first tried to wean her from this love of hers. He felt it did not behove a disciple of the Guru to find pleasure in such frippery. But then he realized that this was the only pleasure in life that she permitted herself. In everything else, she lived her life strictly according to the Guru's precepts. He also realized that having been denied the comfort and blessing of a child, she perhaps found emotional strength and a sense of security in her jewellery collection. Thus, his accepting this foible of hers would be a small concession to make in the face of all that she brought to their marriage and to her dedication and devotion to their Guru and his teachings. She was a great help and support, a helpmate in the true sense of the word.

She came from an extremely well-to-do family herself and her parents and her brothers, recognizing the one material thing that seemed to bring her happiness, showered her with presents of exquisite jewellery. As a result, she had a fabulous collection and wore exquisite items from this collection whenever an opportunity offered itself.

One day, a traveller came to Kartarpur to seek the Guru's blessings and, as so often happened, could find no place to live. 'Go to Moola's house,' he was advised. 'He welcomes people by day and night. Everyone who comes away from his house comes away having been well fed and well looked after.'

It was as he had been told. Moola and his wife welcomed him with open arms and made him comfortable. As luck would have it, a week after his arrival in their house, Moola's wife had to attend a wedding. He saw her adorned in all her finery and took special note of the exquisite and expensive jewellery that she wore that day – the *naulakha*[45] a necklace that came till her waist, the heavy earrings that touched her shoulders and the bracelets and bangles that covered her entire forearms.

Being from a poor background, the sight of so much gold stirred a veritable storm of greed in the traveller's breast. When the lady returned from the wedding that

Moola Keer and the Jewel Thief

night, the traveller lay on his cot, his face covered with a bedsheet, pretending to be asleep. But ever since his hostess had left for the wedding, his mind had thought of nothing else but her jewellery and of how he could get hold of it. Given these thoughts, it was not surprising that he had not been able to sleep. As surreptitiously as he could, he followed her into an inner room and saw her take a wooden box out of a cupboard, take off her jewellery, place it in the box and then place the box back in the cupboard. He knew then with absolute certainty that his greed would not be denied.

He waited long enough for the members of the household to go to sleep. Then, he stole into the inside room, took the wooden box out of the cupboard and stuffed all the jewellery into his undershirt. He then went and woke up his host.

'I had forgotten that tomorrow some people are coming to see my sister with a proposal of marriage. I must be on my way immediately, otherwise I will never reach in time,' he said to Moola.

Moola, now wide awake, looked at his guest in the light of the oil lamp that still burnt on a stand besides his bed and said: 'Under the circumstances, all I can do is to wish you Godspeed. This is one occasion that you must not miss at any cost.'

He reached under his pillow and drew out his bunch of keys, picked up the lamp and the duo made their way to the main gate. 'You must come again to Kartarpur soon,' said Moola.

The traveller, fearing discovery, made no attempt to

thank his host and felt only the need to hurry away as quickly as he could. This very haste was his undoing. He stumbled on the doorstep and the heavy jewellery that he had been hiding, fell to the ground, the gold glittering brightly in the light of the lamp. He looked down at the jewellery and was seized with such a strong feeling of shame that he did not dare to look at his host.

Moola put his arm around the thief's shoudlers. And said: 'Come, my friend, let us find you a sturdy bag so that you can carry your jewellery safely on your journey, without fear of it slipping out of your grasp again.'

There was no irony, no mockery in his voice and when the thief did finally look up into his host's face, all that he saw was the usual kindness, the usual desire to be of service to his guest. He fumbled for words, fumbled for something to express how sorry he was about what he had done. But no words would come.

Moola found a bag into which he put all the jewellery and said: 'Here, now your jewellery is safe. You can carry it without fear of dropping it again.'

Tears welled up in the traveller's eyes. He fell at Moola's feet and wept with sobs that wracked his entire body. 'Forgive me,' he said, between his sobs. 'You have treated me more kindly than anyone has ever treated me in my life and yet I have repaid your kindness with the worst form of ingratitude.'

Moola drew the man to his feet.

'We are mere mortals,' Moola said in a gentle voice. 'As mortals we are susceptible to moments of weakness, moments when, in spite of our convictions, we fall prey to temptation. Your need is obviously very great – much greater than mine.'

He drew the traveller into a close hug and said: 'The jewellery is yours now. Make the best use of it. Use it to set your feet on the path of virtue and goodness and the gold will have proved to be of far greater worth than it was when it was in my wife's cupboard.'

He put his hand on his guest's head and said: 'There is one thing I would ask of you. Do not tell anyone of this incident. Promise me this. I do not want anyone to be able to say that a follower of Nanak had given way to such weakness. Will you promise me this?'

The thief could only nod his head. Words failed him.

'Go, my friend and God be with you always,' said Moola.

Dawn broke. The household stirred and it was not long before the theft was discovered. Moola's wife was distraught.

'How could this have happened?' she asked.

'Our guest remembered that the boy's family was coming to see his sister with a proposal of marriage and had to hurry away. I was so tired and sleepy that I went back to bed without relocking the door. A thief must have taken advantage of the situation and come quietly into the house and stolen your jewellery.'

Moola's wife mulled over her husband's words and believed every one of them.

'Don't worry. I will buy you replacements for each of the pieces you have lost and you will have the added satisfaction of having got rid of your old-fashioned jewellery and come into the possession of a new set, which is in vogue.'

Moola's wife got her new jewellery and the whole of Kartarpur came to believe Moola's version of what had happened and the incident was soon a thing of the past.

However, there was one person who couldn't forget and was kept awake all night, haunted by the hurt he had inflicted on a man who had always remained kind and generous. As the days slid by, he was convinced of the need to redeem himself. He knew there was only one possible way in which he could do it – he must return to Kartarpur and, in full public hearing, confess his crime to the Guru and beg for an opportunity for atonement and redemption.

He followed the dictates of his conscience and returned to Kartarpur. Moola was surprised to see his former guest sitting in a prominent place during the prayer session. When the *kirtan* had been performed and it was time to disperse, the thief came to Nanak with the jewellery bundled up in a piece of cloth. He unbundled it at Nanak's feet and told his story.

When the narrative was over, Nanak scanned the gathering for Moola and, catching sight of him, beckoned him to his side.

'Did you feel no anger when you caught this man in the act of stealing your wife's jewellery?' asked Nanak.

Moola thought for while and then shook his head and

said: 'No, Guruji. I felt no anger or passion. I only felt a little sad that his need was so great that it had made him succumb to the temptation of stealing.'

'How are you so sure it was not pure greed that motivated him?' Nanak asked.

Again, Moola pondered over the Guru's question before he replied: 'No Guruji, I am sure it was not greed. Someone who has been your disciple cannot be motivated by greed alone to do what he knows is wrong. There has to be the compulsion of a pressing need. And, in this case, I suspect it was the need to provide for his sister's wedding.'

The thief held out the jewellery to Moola attempting to restore it to its rightful owner. Moola brushed the offer gently aside and said: 'It is yours now and if your conscience still troubles you, look upon it as a wedding gift for your sister.'

Nanak smiled indulgently at Moola and then, placing his hand on his shoulder, said: 'You have overcome all anger, all passion and even after you have been wronged you have not found it in your heart to condemn the wrongdoer. You have proved, in your desire to protect both the name of this person and the honour of the community, that you deserve the greatest esteem and honour, one that is due only to the most highly evolved men.'

Over the years that followed, Moola displayed his intense devotion to the service of the community again and again.

According to one source:

> They [the followers of Guru Nanak] consider rendering service in the name of the Guru to their own people and to others as the highest form of worship. If a stranger or even a thief or a robber were to call at their door at midnight and seek shelter in the name of their Guru, they would serve him as a friend and brother to the best of their capacity.
>
> – Sujan Rai Bhandari[46]

In holy company, Thy praise I chant.
Thou art shatterer of ignorance, annuller of darkness,
Lofty, inaccessible, immeasurable,
Such is the objective Nanak seeks.
Lord! To the self-alienated grant union
Bringer of all blessings [that] shall be the day,
When the holy Perceptor's feet I touch.

– *Raag Tilang*[47]

Chapter 18

THE IMPOSTOR

𝒩anak's father Mehta Kalu must have had no small measure of gratification during his final years to see that Pandit Hardyal's prophecy had been fulfilled in more than ample measure. Many of the disciples who flocked to Kartarpur and made their homes in the *dera* went on to become legends. Bhai Gurdas, in one of his poems, gives us the names of many of them, prominent among them being Baba Budha, who lived to the ripe old age of 125 (6 October 1506 to 8 September 1631) and witnessed the stewardship of the next five Gurus – Angad (Guru from 1539 to 1552), Amar Das (Guru from 1552 to 1574), Ram Das (Guru from 1574 to 1581), Arjan Dev (Guru from 1581 to 1606) and Har Gobind (Guru from 1606 to 1644).

During this period, the Guru made one last trip, this time an extremely short one – south-east across the Ravi, to Achal – a little village near the town of Batala in Gurdaspur district of Punjab. It had an ancient temple dedicated to Lord Shiva's son, Kartikya, and the village came into its own during the celebration of Maha Shivratri (the great night of Shiva), a Hindu festival celebrated every year in reverence of Lord Shiva. It is the day Shiva was married to Parvati.

Holy men of every hue came to attend the fair at Achal. When word spread of Nanak's arrival, he became the focus of all attention. People gathered in large numbers to seek his blessings and the holy men drew him into discussions to better understand the religious and philosophical stand that he had taken and which had made such a tremendous impact on people from all parts of the country and beyond and from all walks of life.

On his return, Nanak passed a little village. As he walked through it, he remarked upon the fact that the houses were all deserted and there was not a soul to be seen.

'They have perhaps all gone to Achal to attend the Maha Shivratri fair,' suggested Bhai Budha.

However, soon they noticed that at the other end of the village every man, woman and child had crowded around a sadhu who sat in meditation. Nanak and his disciples took their place at the edge of the crowd and discovered, over the next few minutes, that the sadhu was highly respected for his occult powers. It was said that, through the power of his third eye, he could look into his supplicant's future.

After reciting numerous mantras, the sadhu opened his eyes and, reaching forward, picked up a little twig lying in front of him. It was then that Nanak noticed that there were dozens of leaves, twigs, stones and strings of beads, which the villagers had placed in front of the sadhu.

Picking up the little twig, the sadhu held it aloft and one of the villagers got up from the crowd and came and stood in front of him.

'You are in trouble, serious trouble,' he said.

The villager nodded his head.

'The trouble is in your home.' It was more a question than a statement and the villager nodded his head in agreement.

'It is trouble with members of your family.' Again, it was more a question than a statement and again the villager nodded his head in agreement.

'You must recite the Gayatri Mantra[48] ten thousand times and you must make a *godaan* (the gift of a cow) to a Brahmin,' said the sadhu.

The villager moved closer to the sadhu and put a few silver coins in the copper vessel that the sadhu had placed in front of him.

He closed his eyes again and began to recite a series of mantras. After some time, he opened his eyes and the whole procedure was repeated.

On the fourth occasion, a villager sitting in the front of the crowd, realized that the sadhu's copper vessel was placed precariously on the very edge of the platform and, with the weight of the coins that were being placed as offerings in it, was in danger of toppling over the edge. Very quietly, he got to his feet and as gently and unobtrusively as he could he picked up the vessel and placed it to one side, a little outside the sadhu's line of vision.

When the sadhu next opened his eyes, he was shocked to see that the vessel was missing.

'Where is my vessel?' he said his voice loaded with anger. 'Who has stolen my money?'

The villager who had moved the vessel pointed to it.

The sadhu moved it once again to where he could see it and resumed his ministrations. At this point in the proceedings, Nanak got to his feet and, with a smile at his disciples and an incline of his head, indicated that they should move on. As the little group moved away some of the villagers recognized Nanak, and a murmur went around the crowd: 'Nanak is here.'

The village headman rose and touched Nanak's feet as the people crowded around him seeking his blessings. Piqued at losing the attention of the villagers, the sadhu picked up his vessel, now heavy with coins, and made his way from the village.

Nanak turned to the headman and asked: 'Who was this sadhu who drew all of you out of your homes?'

'He is a yogi from Benaras who comes here once a year at Shivratri. He is an extremely learned man and blessed with great occult powers. His third eye is so powerful that he can look into our very souls and identify our troubles, for which he offers us solutions.'

'And the same powerful third eye could not show him that the position of his container of coins had been changed?' Nanak asked.

The villagers looked at each other. Yes, if the sadhu's powerful third eye could look into their very souls, could look into their future, surely it should have had the power to show him that the placement of the copper vessel had been changed. As always, Nanak's logic was simple but irrefutable.

'Do not credit anyone with occult powers. Only one person can control that and it is the Supreme Being.

Address Him, and only Him, when you are seeking help for your troubles. The only magic that exists in the world is the magic that lies in prayer and in acts of charity and piety. It is the only magic that you should invoke and the only magic that will work,' said Nanak to the villagers.

When he finally got up to wend his way home to Kartarpur, it was with the conviction that a majority of the villagers had lost their faith in the hocus pocus of so-called occult powers and the 'magic' that people like the sadhu claimed to be able to perform.

How then light the lamp when there is no oil?
Let your body be the lamp
From the holy books take the wisdom
And use it as oil.
Let knowledge of His presence be the wick
And with the tinder of truth
Light the spark.
Thus light the oil lamp
And in its light meet your Lord.

When the recording Angel claims your body
And catalogues your deeds,
Your good acts will save you from the cycle
of birth and death.
If in life you have served others
Your reward shall be a place in His court,
Says Nanak, you will raise your arms in joy.

– *Raag Sri*[49]

Chapter 19

Mud that Turned to Saffron

Seva was an integral and essential part of the way of life that Nanak sought for his followers. Put simply, *seva* was voluntary service, physical or otherwise, undertaken for the welfare of the community with no regard for reward or recognition of any kind.

The privilege of performing *seva* was sought eagerly by the members of the community and the more menial the task, the more it was prized. But if truth were told, many disciples faltered in performing *seva* in the true sense of the word because, at times, they hoped that their *seva* would be noticed and thus recognized by the master and, if the *seva* was not noticed by Nanak, it would surely be taken note of by God.

There were some truly blessed souls though who always performed *seva* in a true manner. They had obviously been singled out by God for his special benediction. Among these favoured souls was a disciple by the name of Lehna.

Lehna belonged to the village of Khadur (now in district Amritsar) and had, in the years before he became a devotee of Nanak, been a worshipper of the Goddess Durga.[50] During the Navratras,[51] he used to take great pleasure and delight in leading a group of pilgrims from Khadur to Jwalamukhi (now in Himachal Pradesh). The excitement of the pilgrimage had always made him restless, and when the pilgrimage culminated in the darshan or sighting of the Goddess, he had always been filled with ecstasy. But on that particular occasion, he remembered that when the head priest of the temple had finally brought him into the presence of the Goddess, he did not feel the ecstatic happiness that he had always felt before. There was a feeling of inadequacy, a feeling that there should have been something more. This feeling of inadequacy persisted long after he had returned from the pilgrimage and resulted in a restlessness which haunted him in everything that he did. As a result, the following year, he felt none of the excitement that he had felt in each of the previous years, while preparing for the pilgrimage to Jwalamukhi.

It was five in the morning. Lehna had got out of bed, bathed and sat under the tamarind tree in his courtyard to meditate and pray. This had been his daily habit since so long that his wife, Khivi, no longer knew when he stole out of bed. Sitting under the tree, he felt the restlessness return and was not able to concentrate on his prayers. He felt scared. Then, suddenly from his neighbour's courtyard, he heard a soft, clear voice raised in song that went '*Ek Omkar, Satnam, Karta Purakh* ....' It was a strange hymn but the words brought, at last, a measure of peace to his tormented mind and, when the singer finished his song, Lehna was not scared or restless any more. From his neighbour Jodha he learnt that the hymn was called the *mool mantra* and the poet was the great Guru Nanak of Kartarpur.

A few days later, the group of pilgrims led by Lehna tied bells to their wrists and their ankles and set out on their pilgrimage to Jwalamukhi, singing and dancing all the way. But every time they clapped their hands and stamped their feet and chanted '*Jai mata di*', Lehnga would hear a soft, sweet voice rise between the chants and recite '*Ek Omkar, Satnam, Karta Purakh ...* '[52]

The group of pilgrims reached Kartarpur and Lehna refused to go any further. He had found his destination, his Guru, the solace and joy he had long been seeking. His fellow pilgrims reminded him that according to their religious traditions, he, who having made a holy vow but abandoned all efforts to accomplish it, was one of the greatest sinners in the world and would forfeit all his wealth and, if he had sons, they would be taken from him. But Lehna only smiled at these dire warnings and said: 'So be it. If that is the price I shall be called upon to pay for abandoning my pilgrimage and staying on in Kartarpur, I am more than willing to pay it.'

Within a few days, it was as if Lehna had always been in Kartarpur. Wherever there was work to be done, Lehna was the first to reach out. No task was too lowly or too menial for him to perform.

He was in the fields from the break of dawn till the gathering of dusk and, when there was a lull in the agricultural activity, he was happy to serve as a labourer at a construction site or else to work in the community kitchen. In the summer, he would sit fanning the people while they ate their meal and, after the evening meal, while others had gone to bed, he would still happily toil in the *langar*, washing and stacking the utensils. All the time that he worked, he sang his Guru's Bani softly to himself, his mind on the Guru's words, till the words became a part of him.

He was very content to live in the shadow of his Guru, to sit quietly on the fringe of the crowd and take in the beauty of his Guru's teachings. He had no desire to seek the Guru out or to even be noticed by the Guru. But with his selfless and unstinting service, it was inevitable that the Guru would notice him.

One evening, accompanied by Baba Budha and some of his other disciples on his way to the evening satsang, Nanak crossed Lehna, who stood with bowed head and folded hands, waiting for the Guru to pass. But Nanak stopped where Lehna stood and placed his hand on his bowed head.

'Who are you?' he asked, in the gentlest of tones. 'And where do you come from?'

For a moment Lehna stood there, not daring to speak. The Guru had placed his hand on his head and spoken to him. He felt such deep joy that he was afraid to speak, lest the magical spell be broken. At last he spoke.

'I come from Khadur,' he said in a soft voice. 'My name is Lehna.'

'Lehna,' the Guru said, running the name softly off his tongue. 'Whose *lehna* [debt]?' Nanak asked, playing on the meaning of Lehna's name.

Lehna did not understand at first. 'Your *lehna*, your debt, was here, to me in Kartarpur and God has sent you to pay that debt.'

The days slid into weeks and the weeks into months and the months, in turn, into years. Lehna worked diligently each day to repay his debt to the Guru by working tirelessly and selflessly in the service of the *sangat*, the assembly of devotees and disciples. Each night, he went to bed happy in the thought that he had done the most that he could do, the best that he could do. He sought no reward, no special mark of favour from the Guru. But it was only a matter of time before everyone recognized the special nature of the man and of his *seva*. Even though Lehna himself never attached any importance to the fact that the Guru always had a kind word for him, others did, and it was generally recognized that he had a special place in the Guru's heart.

Lehna had always shown consideration and love for his parents, his wife and children. Now that he was away from them, he did not forget them. He sent messages to his father as often as he could. Both Pheru, his father, and Khivi, his wife, had known that there was something different and special about Lehna and were not surprised when he decided to dedicate his life to the service of his Guru and of the *sangat*. Khivi knew that her husband was a good man and that what he was doing was very special. So like Sulakhini, Nanak's wife before her, she prepared to wait out the time till her husband returned to her.

Sometimes, Pheru would accompany Jodha on his visits to Kartarpur to see how his son was faring. Occasionally, he would invite his daughter-in-law to come with him. Short as these visits were, Khivi was happy to be with her husband again.

One day, after the morning prayers, the Guru sent for Lehna.

'You have paid your debt to me well,' the Guru said, referring to their first conversation three years ago. 'But there are other debts you still must pay: the debt to your father, the debt to your wife and children. You must return to Khadur and settle your affairs.'

The story of Lehna's service and the favour he had received had travelled to Khadur. When the news spread that Lehna had returned, people came to greet him in large numbers. There was love and affection for a good, kind man who had been away from home for three long years and there was respect for the man who had come so close to the master.

Lehna spent some time in arranging his affairs and, when he was sure that he had made sufficient provisions for his parents, his wife and his children, he said goodbye to them and returned to Kartarpur.

There was a heavy and prolonged downpour on the way and he took shelter in a dilapidated hut, resuming his journey when the rain finally stopped. He reached Kartarpur in the early hours of the evening when the sun was setting. Stopping only to stable his horse, he hurried to the fields where he knew the Guru would be at work. The Guru greeted him warmly and, when Lehna looked around to see what task remained, he found that all that remained to be done was to carry home some bundles of freshly cut fodder.

'I'll go home and send one of the *sevadars* with bullock-carts to carry the fodder home,' said Lakhmi Das, Nanak's younger son. He obviously did not wish to soil his clothes by carrying the fodder himself. Lehna, without a word, lifted the bundles onto his head, one upon the other, and made his way through the fields towards the Guru's home. The fodder was wet, dripping wet, and the muddy water dripped from his head, over his neck and down to his shirt, which was soon covered with smudges. It was a beautiful shirt, made from *boski* (Chinese silk), which Khivi had bought from a trader. No one in the village had a shirt as beautiful as this and she was proud that she had given her husband something so beautiful. He, who cared nothing for wordly things, had teased her about it.

'When will I ever need to wear something so grand?'

'When you return to Kartarpur and go to meet your Guru,' his wife had replied.

That was how he had worn this special shirt for his journey to Kartarpur. And here it was now, sticking to his back, soiled and dirty. But he did not notice it. He was happy to be performing a service for his Guru. It was Sulakhini who noticed that the shirt had been spoilt. The moment she saw Lehna approaching the house with the load of fodder on his head, she took the Guru aside and berated him.

'How could you do this?' she asked. 'How could you allow Lehna to carry this load and dirty his clothes with mud?'

'When the mud comes from such willing and selfless service it no longer remains mud,' Guru Nanak replied, smiling quietly at his wife. 'It becomes saffron. And when the load of fodder is carried by Lehna, it is no longer a load of fodder but the halo of God's blessing.'

When Sulakhini turned and looked again at Lehna, she indeed thought that she saw a circle of light around his head.

The monsoon had broken in its full fury and, in the middle of the night, word was brought to the Guru that one of the walls of the newly built wing of the *dharamshala* was about to give way. The Guru hurried to see the extent of the damage. He found a handful of disciples already there and amongst them, unsurprisingly, Lehna. Part of the wall had indeed given way and, unless something was done to shore it up immediately, the entire wall was in danger of coming down.

Nanak turned to his son Lakhmi Das and said: 'Son, this needs to be attended to immediately.'

'Yes father,' Lakhmi Das said stifling a yawn. 'As soon as the first light breaks I will find the masons and have it attended to.'

The little group dispersed. But Lehna returned quietly and surveyed the extent of the damage. His Guru had said that it needed to be attended to immediately and his Guru's word was law. He went out to look for the regular masons. The few that could be found, not wishing to work in such inclement weather, pleaded ill health. The only help he could find was a wizened old mason, no longer capable of working himself, who offered to supervise what needed to be done. Lehna persuaded four other disciples to help him and scrounged all the material that the 'expert' said they would need.

Hour after hour through that long, stormy night, Lehna and his companions struggled under the directions of the 'expert' to contain the damage that had been done by the rain. On at least two occasions, when they were nearing the end of their work, the 'expert' said it would have to be done all over again. The others groaned and threatened to leave, but Lehna smiled encouragingly and cheered them on. A little before dawn, they were done and the danger had been averted.

When Nanak stopped to take stock of the situation on his way to the morning prayers, he saw that timely action had averted the danger. Now, the masons could take over and do whatever they thought was necessary. When he asked who had been responsible for repairing the damaged wall, it came as no surprise to him to be told that it was Lehna who had led the work and toiled hour after hour at the wall.

By now there were strong rumours that Nanak would choose Lehna as his successor. His older son Sri Chand was not an ambitious man and, though spiritually inclined, did not aspire to succeed his father. He was a pious man and there were those who felt that it would be in the fitness of things if he were to succeed Nanak as the Guru. Nanak was aware of this feeling and knew he had to take immediate steps to stall the formation of factions.

He called for a meeting with his sons and with some of the senior and well-respected members of the *sangat*.

He addressed Lehna and said: 'Bhai Lehna you have shown through your selfless service over these long years that you are the flesh of my flesh and blood of my blood. You are an *ang* [part] of my body.'

Lehna caught Baba Budha's eye and the Baba smiled. 'Because you are a part of me you are best suited to carry forward the work that I have begun. Come Bhai Budha, come and apply saffron paste on Lehna's forehead.'

Then he placed five copper coins and a coconut at Lehna's feet and bowed to him. Thus, Lehna was ordained as the second Guru of the Sikhs, Guru Angad Dev. Nanak had called him his *ang*, a part of himself. From this was derived the name Angad that he was given when he was anointed.

Without good deeds both lead only to suffering,
Neither Hindu nor Muslim finds refuge in God's Court.

— *Var 1:33*[53]

Chapter 20
There Is No Hindu, No Mussalman

The years had taken their toll and, almost all those whom Nanak had loved and held dear to his heart, had been sifted out of his life by the sieve of time. His mentor and friend Rai Bular, his father Mehta Kalu, mother Tripta, his sister Nanki and her husband Jai Ram, and even Mardana, whose multifaceted relationship with the Guru defied a label or a name, had been taken away from him. Nanak, tired and frail from the rigours of the life he had led, knew it was now time for him to go too.

As he lay under a tree on the bank of the river Ravi, just outside Kartarpur, Angad sat with Nanak's feet in his lap, his heart heavy not only with the grief of the impending end but also with the burden of the responsibilities that he would soon have to shoulder.

All day, people from distant places came to see their Guru one last time. Sometimes, Nanak would close his eyes and sleep, sometimes he would be awake. Though he had some lucid moments, his eyes did not always register those who had come to see him. His breathing was laboured and the end, it was obvious, was near.

The breeze shook the leaves of the tree. The dry ones rattled as they struck one another and fell on the ground. Nanak opened his eyes and looked up at the tree. Then he looked at Angad and smiled. Angad understood the meaning of that smile – the old leaves must fall and make place for the new, just as the old must leave the world to make place for the young. Then the Guru's eyes clouded again and he seemed to lose awareness of the world around him and of the people who sat patiently by his side.

A murmur rose amongst the Guru's Muslim followers who sat to his left. At first, Angad could not make out what was being said. Then, as they raised their voices, he heard the words clearly: 'He is ours, our peer, our holy man. So when he dies his body must be handed over to us so that we can give him holy burial.'

The Hindu followers, who sat to the Guru's right, were very upset by this claim. 'No, no,' they protested. 'Nanak was born a Hindu. His father's name was Kalyan and his mother's name was Tripta. In his teachings, there is a great deal that is common to the Hindu way of life. Besides, he has never said that he is a Mussalman. So how can you say he is yours? He is our Guru and his body will be ours, so that we can give him the cremation rites that all true-born Hindus need to be given.'

The Guru opened his eyes and chuckled softly as Angad held up his hand and the bickering ceased.

'You are both right,' the Guru said in a soft, sympathetic voice, looking first towards one group and then towards the other. 'I belong to both of you. But there is a way out of this dilemma. Each of you must bring flowers, plenty of flowers and put them beside me. The Muslims must lay their flowers along my left and the Hindus along my right. You must leave them there through the night. Then tomorrow, when I am gone, you must both look at your flowers carefully. If the flowers on the side of the Hindus are fresher than the ones along the other side, then I belong to the Hindus and they can cremate my body. But if the flowers along the side of the Muslims are fresher, then I belong to them and they can give me a burial.'

He closed his eyes again and drifted off to sleep. His disciples did as they had been bid. The Hindus brought marigold and red roses and placed them along the right side of the sleeping Guru and the Muslims brought red and pink roses and sweet smelling jasmines and placed them them along the Guru's left side. Then, they sat patiently to wait out the night. Some of them dozed off while others looked into the Guru's face by the light of the oil lamps that burned near his head, their minds filling with memories of the Guru's words and deeds.

It was now only moments before the ambrosial hour, the *amrit vela*. The Guru woke up one last time and, in the faintest of voices, asked his followers to pray. Then, as they recited the *mool mantra*, he drew his sheet over his face and went into eternal sleep. (The date: 22 September 1539.)

All through the morning, his disciples sat beside their Guru, and in the afternoon when it was time to perform the funeral ceremonies, both the Hindus and the Muslims carefully examined the flowers that they had brought for their Guru. The Muslims looked at their roses and the jasmine and found that they were as fresh as when they had brought them. The Hindus looked at their roses and marigold and found that they too had lost none of their freshness. Both sides looked at each other in puzzlement and then, gradually, as understanding dawned on them, their faces broke into radiant smiles. Even in death, Nanak had underscored the lesson that he had taught all his life: All human beings are equal. There is no Hindu, there is no Mussalman.

There are only good, decent men like the Guru who have made the world as beautiful and fresh and sweet smelling as the flowers, with the good deeds that they have performed during their lives.

Notes and References

1. Dr Kirpal Singh: *Janamsakhi Tradition – An Analytical Study*, Singh Brothers, Amritsar, 2004.
2. Ibid., p. 59.
3. In Hinduism, *bhakti* refers to religious devotion of a devotee in the worship of the divine. Within monotheistic Hinduism, it is the love felt by the worshipper towards the personal God, a concept expressed in Hindu theology as *Isa-devatā* – Wikipedia
4. Harbans Singh: Perspectives on Guru Nanak, seminar papers, Punjabi University, Patiala, 1975, p. 79.
5. A dervish is a Muslim religious man or woman who has taken vows of poverty and austerity. Dervishes first appeared in the twelfth century and were noted for their wild or ecstatic rituals. They were known as dancing, whirling, or howling dervishes according to the practice of their order.
6. Kumbh Mela is a mass pilgrimage of faith in which Hindus gather to bathe in a sacred river. It is considered to be the largest peaceful gathering in the world, which around 100 million people visit. It is held every third year at one of the four places by rotation: Haridwar, Allahabad (Prayag), Nashik and Ujjain – Wikipedia.
7. Dattatreya is considered by some Hindus (in western India) to be an incarnation of the Divine Trinity of Brahma, Vishnu and Shiva – Wikipedia.
8. Shankaracharya is a commonly used title for the heads of monasteries called *mathas* (religious orders). The title derives from Adi Shankara, an eighth-century reformer of Hinduism.

The popular view among historians is that there were four *mathas* – north (Jyothirmath), south (Sringeri), east (Puri), and west (Dwarka) – to propagate the philosophy of Advaita Vedanta and to promulgate the concept of Sanatana Dharma, thus establishing dharma or righteousness as a way of life – Wikipedia.

9. K. S. Duggal: *Select Sikh Scriptures*, Vol. I, UBSPD, New Delhi, 1997, p. 90.
10. Kshatriya (a warrior) is one of the four *varnas* (social orders) of the Hindu society. The Sanskrit term Kshatriya is used in the context of Vedic society wherein members organized themselves into four classes: Brahmin, Kshatriya, Vaishya and Shudra – Wikipedia.
11. Khushwant Singh: *A History of the Sikhs,* Vol. I: 1469–1839, Oxford University Press, New Delhi, 1963, p. 345.
12. Bani (short for Gurbani) is the term used for referring to various sections of the Adi Granth or also known as Guru Granth. The word Gurbani consists of two roots – Guru and Bani. The word 'Guru' means spiritual teacher and here refers to the ten Gurus of Sikhism, besides the other teachers and saints whose writings can be found in the holy Guru Granth. The word Banis refers to their utterances and writings.
13. The rabaab, known as 'the lion of instruments', is a short-necked lute whose body is carved out of a single piece of wood, with a membrane covering the hollow bowl of the sound chamber, upon which the bridge is positioned. It has three melody strings tuned in fourths, three drone strings and eleven or twelve sympathetic strings. The instrument is made from the trunk of the mulberry tree, the head from animal skin such as goat, and the strings either from the gut or from the intestines of young goats brought to the size of thread – Wikipedia.
14. Kabir (1440–1518) was a mystic poet and saint, whose writings greatly influenced the Bhakti Movement. His *dohas* (couplets)

are sung even today. The name Kabir comes from Arabic *al-Kabīr*, which means 'The Great' – the thirty-seventh name of God in Islam – Wikipedia.
15. Harbans Singh: op. cit., p. 157.
16. Gomukh – 'mouth of the cow' – the terminus or snout of the Gangotri glacier, from where the Bhagirathi river originates, is one of the primary sources of the river Ganga. It is situated at a height of about 4040 metres or 13,200 feet and is one of the largest glaciers in the Himalayas. It is a popular Hindu pilgrimage site – Wikipedia.
17. Dr Kirpal Singh: op.cit., p. 106.
18. Harbans Singh: *Guru Nanak and Origins of the Sikh Faith*, Asia Publishing House, Bombay, 1969, p. 105.
19. Khushwant Singh: op.cit., p. 332.
20. Wikipedia.
21. Durvasa was an ancient saint who occupies a predominant position in the history of sages. He is believed to have lived in the Satyug, Tretayug and Dwaparyug. He was known for his bad temper. Although he was respected for his knowledge and wisdom, everyone was scared of his anger. He had a habit of cursing people over small mistakes. But his anger was always short-lived and he himself used to tell the remedy to remove the effect of the curse – Source: astrobix religion.
22. As mentioned earlier, Asuras are a group of power-seeking demons related to the more benevolent demigods or Devas (also known as Suras). Asuras battle constantly with the Devas.
23. Indra is the God of rain and thunderstorms and wields a lightning thunderbolt known as *vajra* and rides on a white elephant named Airavata. Indra is the brother of Varuna and Yama – Wikipedia.
24. Varuna is the God of the water and of the celestial ocean as well as of the underwater world.

25. Mount Meru also called Sumeru is a sacred mountain in Hindu and Buddhist cosmology as well as in Jain cosmology and is considered to be the centre of all the physical, metaphysical and spiritual universes. It is also the abode of Lord Brahma and the Devas. Many famous Hindu and Jain temples have been built as symbolic representations of this mountain.
26. Amavasya means new moon night in Sanskrit and is common to almost all Indian languages as they are all heavily influenced by Sanskrit. Mauni Amavasya occurs on the fifteenth day of the dark fortnight of the month of Magh (January-February). It is derived from the word *muni*, literally means an ascetic who practises silence. Mauni Amavasya is believed to be the day of conjunction of the sun and the moon. Fasting is observed on this day and the devotees do not talk to each other during the observance – Wikipedia and Premastrologer.com.
27. K. S. Duggal: op.cit., p. 215.
28. Khushwant Singh: op.cit., p. 351.
29. Khushwant Singh: *Japjee – The Sikh Morning Prayer*, Picus Books, New Delhi, 1999, p. 123.
30. In the Mahabharata, a Hindu epic text, the Pandavas are the five sons of Pandu, by his two wives Kunti and Madri. Their names are Yudhisthira, Bhima, Arjuna, Nakula and Sahadeva. Together, the brothers fought and prevailed in a great war against their cousins the Kauravas, which came to be known as the Battle of Kurukshetra.
31. K. S. Duggal: op.cit., p. 133.
32. Baisakhi is the harvest festival for Punjabis and, according to the Punjabi calendar, the Punjabi New Year. The Punjabi calendar is based on the Bikrami calendar. This day is also observed as the thanksgiving day by the farmers whereby they pay their tribute, thanking God for the abundant harvest and also praying for future prosperity.
33. Few figures from the Indian past strike most Hindus with as much revulsion as the conqueror Mahmud of Ghazni, who

succeeded his father, a warlord who had carved out an empire in central Asia and had established his capital at Ghazni, south of Kabul, in A.D. 998, at the age of twenty-seven. He launched aggressive expansionist campaigns and is said to have invaded India no less than seventeen times between A.D. 1000 and 1025. His invasions of India, which never extended to the central, south and eastern portions of the country, were doubtless exceedingly bloody and ruthless affairs. He is said to have carried away huge amount of booty on each visit – sscnet.ucla.edu/southasia/History.
34. See sscnet.ucla.edu/southasia/History.
35. Source: Wikipedia.
36. Harbans Singh: *Guru Nanak and the Origins of the Sikh Faith*, Asia Publishing House, New Delhi, 1969, p. 156.
37. The *gurukul* is a traditional residential school where students stay and study along with the guru/s. It came into existence during the Vedic period.
38. K. S. Duggal: op.cit., p. 206.
39. Amarnath cave, a Hindu shrine located in Kashmir and dedicated to Lord Shiva, has been a place of worship since time immemorial. Situated at an altitude of 3888 metres (or 12,756 feet), about 140 km from Srinagar, it is considered to be one of the holiest shrines in Hinduism. It is covered with snow most of the year, except for a short period during summers when it is open for pilgrims. This 40-metre (130-foot)-high cave has a stalagmite which is formed due to freezing of water drops that fall from the roof of the cave on to the floor that grows up vertically, thus taking the form of a Shiva *lingam* (in the symbolic shape of a phallus). As per the religious beliefs, the *lingam* grows and shrinks with the phases of the moon, reaching its maximum height during the summer festival, although there is no scientific evidence for this belief. According to a Hindu legend, this is the cave where

Shiva explained the secret of life and eternity to his divine consort, Parvati. – Wikipedia.
40. With an impressive height of 6638 metres (or 21,778 feet), the legendary Mount Kailash (now in Tibet) represents the axis of the world or the stairway to heaven for the people in the region. Both Buddhists and Hindus recognize it as an ancient holy place. It is indeed an axis, if only because it is the source of major Asian rivers, including the Indus.
41. Khushwant Singh: *A History of the Sikhs*, Vol. I: 1469-1839, Oxford University Press, New Delhi, 1963, p 47.
42. Bhai Sikander Singh (tr.): *Nanak's azaan from Bhai Mani Singh's Janamsakhis* (publishing details not available).
43. K. S. Duggal: op.cit., p. 149.
44. Khushwant Singh: *A History of the Sikhs*, Vol. I: 1469-1839; Oxford University Press, New Delhi, 1963, p. 347.
45. *Naulakha*: A precious necklace that is worth Rs 900,000
46. Harbans Singh: *Guru Nanak and the Origins of the Sikh Faith*, Asia Publishing House, New Delhi, 1969.
47. Gurbachan Singh Talib: *Guru Granth Sahib*, Vol I, Punjabi University, Patiala, 1977, p. 281.
48. The Gayatri Mantra is not just a means of worship but is an object of worship in itself. The word 'Gayatri' is used both in reference to the Gayatri Mantra as an object of worship and in reference to the divine entity described in the mantra – Wikipedia.
49. Khushwant Singh: *A History of the Sikhs*, Vol. I: 1469-1839, Oxford University Press, New Delhi, 1963, p. 343.
50. Durga, meaning 'the inaccessible' or 'the invincible', is the most popular incarnation of Devi and one of the main forms of the Goddess Shakti in the Hindu pantheon. Durga is the original manifested form of Mother Parvati – Wikipedia.
51. An important and a major festival celebrated all over India, it is dedicated to the worship of the Hindu Goddess Durga. The word in itself means 'nine nights' in Sanskrit. During

these nine nights and ten days, nine forms of Shakti/Devi are worshipped – Wikipedia.
52. One Universal Creator God/ The Name is truth . . . Creative Being Personified . . . –Wikipedia.
53. W. H. McLeod: *Exploring Sikhism: Aspects of Sikh Identity, Culture, and Thought*, Oxford University Press, New Delhi, 2003, p. 43.

Further Reading*

Dhillon, Harish: *The First Sikh Spiritual Master*, Skylight Paths Publishing, Woodstock, Vermont, USA, 2006.

Dhillon, Harish: *The Lives and Teachings of the Sikh Gurus*, Hay House Publishers India, New Delhi, 2015.

Sarna, Navtej: *The Book of Nanak*, Penguin Books India, New Delhi, 2005.

Singh, Dr Kirpal and Kharak Singh: *History of the Sikhs and Their Religion*, Vol. 1, Dharam Prachar Committee, Shiromani Gurdwara Parbandhak Committee (SGPC), Amritsar, 1994.

*These books are in addition to those already mentioned under Notes and References.

Acknowledgements

First and foremost, my deep and abiding gratitude goes to Ashok Chopra (the CEO and managing director of Hay House Publishers India) for having commissioned this book. I am grateful to Bhim Inder, who, as usual, provided me with all the resource material and appropriate quotations from Nanak's Bani. Thanks, too, to Bhai Sikander Singh for having read the manuscript and providing useful advice and useful material, including the original '*azaan*' for the Music and Worship story. A big thank you to Kuldeep for doing so much running around for the book and helping me give it final shape. Some of the translations of the Bani have been taken from the excellent books by Navtej Sarna, Harbans Singh, Khushwant Singh, K. S. Duggal, Dr Kirpal Singh and Dr Gurbachan Singh Talib and some have been provided by Bhim Inder and Bhai Sikander Singh. Finally, my heartfelt thanks to everyone at Hay House for giving me this excellently produced book, and in particular to Rakesh Kumar for the layout and production and Raghav Khattar for designing the cover.

CONNECT WITH
HAY HOUSE
ONLINE

 hayhouse.co.in   @hayhouseindia

 @hayhouseindia   @hayhouseindia

Join the conversation about latest products, events, exclusive offers, contests, giveaways and more.

'The gateways to wisdom and knowledge are always open.'

Louise Hay

www.ingramcontent.com/pod-product-compliance
Lightning Source LLC
LaVergne TN
LVHW091627070526
838199LV00044B/966